Excerpts:

Trump is the catalyst that has ignited the silent majority into action. Many Americans whose feelings toward minorities and immigrants were dormant for years were jolted into reality by Trump's bigotry. Those who were content to remain silent and remain on the sidelines have found their voice. They will not stand idly by and tolerate Trump's acts of gross inhumanity. The surge of anti-Trump sentiment has produced millions of citizens who are new to politics but want their voices to be heard in efforts to blunt the Trump agenda and work against his re-election. The efficiency in marshalling this force into an effective political movement will determine the outcome of the 2018 and 2020 elections.

To defeat Trump is #1 priority, but more needs to be done. The critical problems facing our nation:
1. Entitlements are under- funded.
2. The Military Budget is obese.
3. Tax structure needs a recast.

Replacing Trump, while it is critical, will not solve these pressing problems. Newly elected legislators must be committed to these issues to enable the long term stability of our country.

The Campaign:

To describe the 2016 Presidential Campaign as a disaster would be gratuitous. We allowed the focus of the news coverage of the candidates to dwell on innuendo and insults, lies and accusation, the more salacious the news, the greater the media coverage. The entire process disintegrated into sound bites and expletives. Is this what America has become? Are we a people driven by their most basic instincts? Where compassion and empathy are overridden by avarice and hatred? Has our democratic system deteriorated to the point where we have to choose which presidential candidate we dislike the least?

"The Elephant in the room"

With the media coverage on the candidate's shortcomings, little attention was paid to the critical issues facing our country. The "elephant in the room," ignored by the candidates and the press is the state of our country's finances. Our yearly Budget Deficit has ranged from one half to one and one half Trillion dollars per year for the past eight years. We have spent more than we earned every year for the past thirty seven years with the exception of four years 1998-2001. This deficit spending has resulted in a negative net worth for the country of over Ten Trillion dollars. We are a strong and vibrant country capable of operating on a profitable basis, but we need to rein in our military and bring their thinking into the 21st Century. Our Defense Department is still operating in the 1900's. We could have an adequate National Defense with one half the current Military Budget. Reworking our Tax System – see pages 126-133 will enable us fund the Military, meet our Entitlement obligations and pay down our debt before the increasing interest rates close our window of opportunity.

The Election:

"I don't think there's ever been two more unlikeable candidates," said Michael Che during the Weekend Update sketch on Saturday Night Live. "Not one time in this election have I heard anyone say: 'You know what? I like them *both*.'"

The data from the Exit Polls conducted by Edison Research for the National Election Pool show Mr. Che to be correct – an extremely small portion of the voting public (only 2%) told our exit pollsters they had a favorable view of both. While most voters did have a favorable view of one of the two major candidates – an astonishing 18% of the electorate told us they had an unfavorable opinion of both Hillary Clinton and Donald Trump.

The Aftermath:

It is a travesty of our American heritage and everything we stand for as a nation to tolerate the dismantling of the freedom and values that have been so dearly won since the creation of this great nation. Yes, let us make America great again, not in the image of Mr. Trump, but an America of inclusiveness, compassion and freedom to pursue ones' dreams. Let us stand up for humanity. We cannot let our entire system fail because of one man.

Our Worst Nightmare:

March 6, 2017: U.S. Strategic Command said North Korea launched four guided missiles from a launch site on North Korea's west coast near the border with China. The missiles flew 600 miles across the country before splashing into the Sea of Japan. In Japan, the government said three of the missiles had landed within 200 miles of their coastline. The most disturbing factor in this exhibition, the Pentagon says North Korea's leader, Kim Jong-Un, is acting more "*irrationally and unpredictably"* than previously.

When you consider two world leaders, half a world apart, sharing similar personality traits, both having the keys to their nuclear arsenals, we must be very afraid for the future of mankind.

The Future:

Candidates for office should be vetted for their stand on inclusion and humanitarianism. We cannot treat our country as an "island fortress". Those seeking a new life should be welcome here.

The mid-term elections in 2018 are crucial to forming a beachhead against the prevailing political structure. Finding candidates, male and female, with the "balls" to fight the establishment will be challenging, but an absolute necessity.
How do persons who were motivated to demonstrate convert those energies into political action?
> 1. **You need a plan.**
> 2. **You need people to implement the plan.**
> 3. **You need to see it through to conclusion.**

The Plan:

*Obtain control of Congress in the 2018 elections and the White House in 2020.

*Join or create an organization to fight for redistricting where needed. Persevere, do the tedious follow through work.

*Vet potential congressional candidates in regard to their fervor for supporting humanitarianism, a modern military and debt reduction.

*Seek the help of your friends to keep the pressure on.

*Enlist candidates who can win elections for congressional seats in 2018 and support their candidacy. Get out the vote!

*Support the independent thinkers on both sides of the aisle.

*Seek out Republican Congressional members who have aligned themselves against Trump and help them be reelected.

Table of Contents

Published 2017

ISBN 978-0-9829136-4-2

Fuck. Now what?

Preface

F**K

We elected the "school yard bully" to be our President.

Now what?

Clearly, our system is broken. Trump is but a symbol of how the political parties have been bullying the electorate for decades. We have allowed our politicians to dictate their agenda to us rather than listening to us. How did this happen? As a citizenry, we became complacent and failed to make our voices heard. This is changing, as evidenced by the "Women's March on Washington". The protest drew huge crowds across the nation and the world with an estimated four and one half million protesters in the U.S. alone, making it the largest protest in our history.

The major problem: how to convert this energy into action to produce meaningful results. If there is to be significant change, it should be accomplished within the framework of our political system. That means starting from the bottom up and working for change at every level. Grass roots organizations such as *Women4Change Indiana* and *Count MI Vote* in Michigan have attracted members who are avidly advocating change in their states.

"The Future" section of this book delves into what can be done to mitigate the damage from Trump's actions until the "mid-term" elections. If our work proves effective, we will elect congressional members who can stand up to Trump and vote their conscience. By 2020, we can elect a President who can end this travesty and begin the process of returning our country to its values.

Fighting for change isn't easy, and recently in Indiana, which is a poster child for Gerrymandering, the Elections and Apportionment Committee Chairman, Milo Smith, refused to allow a vote on a motion to introduce a bill that would have appointed an independent commission for redistricting the state. The hearing was packed with hundreds of supporters of the bill but Smith turned a deaf ear to their advocacy. Grass roots effort to un-elect Milo Smith is how citizens exert their rights.

Political activism is fraught with roadblocks and disappointment, and only the hardy persevere. The entrenched establishment fights for their status quo at every step in the process and movements such as Count MI Vote who advocate "**Voters should chose their politicians, not the other way around**", have to navigate around many potholes on the road to redistricting.

Visit to the Gerald R. Ford:

How ironic! Our *Egomaniac-in Chief* used his visit to the new 13 Billion dollar aircraft carrier, the Gerald R. Ford, to promote a 54 Billion increase in the Defense budget. There is nothing more symbolic of the antiquated thinking of our military establishment than this floating island. When, and if, all three of this class of carriers were built, the price tag, including development, will be north of 45 Billion dollars.
What is it about these floating islands that make our military believe they will be invisible to surveillance satellites? One guided missile launch and poof, it's all over for thousands of lives.
Our military budget is already too high, and Trump wants to increase it another 54 Billion? This is insane! If we reduced our budget by 250 Billion, it would still exceed the combined military budgets of Russia and China.
Hopefully, his intention to decimate the foreign aid and humanitarian budgets to pay for his toys will be shot down in Congress.

The Campaign:

We should have seen meaningful discussions about the issues facing our nation:

> 1. The growing cost of entitlements.
>
> 2. A military establishment that is grossly overweight.
>
> 3. The National Debt.
>
> 4. A society torn by ethnic and economic divisiveness.

We saw:

> 1. Negativity.
>
> 2. Charges of corruption
>
> 3. Charges of misogyny
>
> 4. Personal attacks.

What happened? – What should have happened, and where do we go from here?

What were we thinking? We weren't thinking at all. Rather than debating the pressing issues of the day, we became immersed in basic instincts from the ridiculous to the prurient. We were inundated with negativity, by so many onerous ads, so many reasons to NOT vote for a candidate. Instead of insisting on a debate over meaningful issues such as Health Care, entitlements, national debt and national security, we heard remarks about a candidate's physical stature or personality.

To describe the 2016 Presidential Campaign as a disaster would be gratuitous. We allowed the focus of the news coverage of the candidates to dwell on innuendo and insults, lies and accusation, the more salacious the news, the greater the media coverage. The entire process disintegrated into sound bites and expletives.

We did not insist on substantive issues to be presented to the candidates, but allowed the coverage to degrade into discussion of the candidates hand size, presumably as an indicator of their manliness. There was so much negativity it was difficult to determine what the candidates were advocating. The policy pronouncements that were made were buried under a sea of sludge. "Crooked Hillary" and Trumps "Just grab 'em by the P***y" so dominated the campaign that voters were left with making a decision without any clear understanding of what either candidate was actually promising.

There has never been a presidential campaign that was more about personalities and less about issues facing our nation. The candidate's views on the size and use of our military, their concept of how to deal with the mushrooming entitlement programs and the national debt were hardly discussed.

Following is an excerpt from the 11th Republican candidates' debate in Detroit, MI on March 3rd, 2016

TRUMP: Well, I also happened to call him a lightweight, OK? And I have said that. So I would like to take that back. He is really not that much of a lightweight. And as far as -- and I have to say this, I have to say this. He hit my hands. Nobody has ever hit my hands. I have never heard of this. Look at those hands. Are they small hands?
(LAUGHTER)
TRUMP: And he referred to my hands, if they are small, something else must be small. I guarantee you there is no problem. I guarantee.

This is the first reference to a penis that has been made in a presidential debate and is indicative of the overall tone of the debates. Substance was scarce, insult and innuendo was the norm. Unfortunately, this nastiness carried over to the Clinton-Trump debates.

Clinton, Trump Debates:

The first debate:

Clinton referred to Trumps denigrating attitude toward women by bringing up Alicia Machado, Miss Universe of 1996, who said Trump tried to humiliate her after she gained weight.

"He called me Miss Piggy, Miss Housekeeping" said Machado.

Miss Machado's story is just one example of Trumps' misogyny. A more lurid example would surface later.

The second debate:

Just three days before the debate, Trumps "Grab 'em by the p***y remark hit the news media.

When Clinton questioned Trumps attitude toward women, he responded by saying "There's never been anybody in the history of politics in this nation that's been so abusive to women as Bill Clinton". He denied sexually assaulting women and said his remarks were "locker room talk" and deflected questions by stating that he would attack the Islamic State and saying "When I am president we will have a special prosecutor to look into Hillary".

The third debate:

Most notable in this debate was Trumps assertion that if he won, he would accept the verdict of the voters in the November 8 election, but if he lost, he would not say if he would accept that verdict and the system could be rigged.

 CNN asked their commentators and guest analysts to express their opinions regarding the debate and of the 18 who wrote of their impressions from the debate, 17 commented they expected a Clinton victory in the election and had serious misgivings regarding Trumps ability and temperament for the job of President.

The following is an excerpt from comments by Frida Ghitis, Columnist World Politics Review, Miami Herald: *Reprinted with permission

"If you're not frightened for America, you have not been paying attention. That was clear even in this final debate, in which Donald Trump managed to keep his cool for about the first 30 to 45 minutes, appearing to maintain control over his baser instincts. The effort to restrain himself proved too strenuous, and he finely dropped all pretense of discipline. We saw the real Trump, and it was a most unpleasant sight.

Nothing Trump does or says comes as a surprise any more. But we should not lose our ability to be shocked. The Republican candidate for the presidency refused to say he would accept the outcome of the election. America's foes, the enemies of democracy around the world, must have rubbed their hands in glee.

One of the great achievements of humanity is the democratic tradition of peaceful transfer of power, the knowledge that after a hard-fought campaign the loser concedes. Trump may

or may not accept that. Forget November 8th. What is he planning for November 9th?

How scary is Trump? Imagine he wins the election. The dark scenarios are endless. But fast-forward to four years later. Imagine that he wins the election. Imagine he runs for re-election and loses, and then refuses to give up power. Trump has the instincts of a dictator.

Some dictators are charming. Trump is not. He lied so many times it was amazing to watch. He claimed the accusations of women against him have been debunked. They have not. He rejected the judgment of US security agencies about Russian hacking in the US.

And then, near the end, in a most revolting moment, he interrupted Clinton to say, "She's a nasty woman."

Trump solidified his standing with his hardcore supporters, promoting what sounds more and more like a seditious movement, a movement to incite rebellion against the lawful government of the United States.

If Trump had maintained discipline, he might have scored some points. Instead, he reminded us what a frightening election this is, what a frightening man he is."

*End of quote

Is there reason to believe he will succeed?

The Election:

Voters clearly were looking for an alternative to what they perceived to be years of political squabbling and deadlock.

Interesting exit polling analysis by **Edison Research** highlights the effect that one category of voters had on the outcome of the election.

The Hidden Group that Won the Election for Trump:

*Reprinted with permission

By: Larry Rosin

"I don't think there's ever been two more unlikeable candidates," said Michael Che during the Weekend Update sketch on Saturday Night Live this week. "Not one time in this election have I heard anyone say: 'You know what? I like them *both*.'"

The data from the Exit Polls conducted by Edison Research for the National Election Pool show Mr. Che to be correct – an extremely small portion of the voting public (only 2%) told our exit pollsters they had a favorable view of both. While most voters did have a favorable view of one of the two major candidates – an astonishing 18% of the electorate told us they had an unfavorable opinion of both Hillary Clinton and Donald Trump. And this is the group that won the election for Trump.

Favorable only to Clinton	41
Favorable only to Trump	36
Favorable to both	2
Favorable to neither	18

edison
research

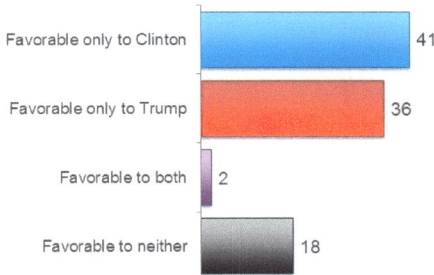

Source: NEP Exit Poll conducted by Edison Research

The fact that nearly one-in-five voters who didn't like either major candidate still came out to vote is pretty remarkable. This number is double what we saw four years ago (9% were unfavorable to both in 2012) and nearly four times what we saw in the Bush-Kerry match-up of 2004 (favorability ratings were not asked in the 2008 exit polls).

As you might expect, if you had a favorable impression of one candidate and not the other, in virtually every case you voted for that one candidate. So had those with a negative view of both candidates split evenly, Clinton would have won rather easily. However, as the graph below shows, this "Neithers" group broke strongly to Trump 47% to 30%.

The "Neithers"

Vote among those unfavorable to both candidates (18%):

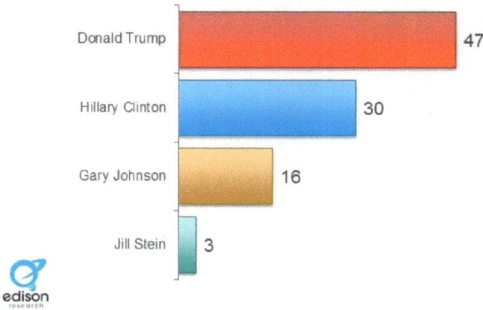

Donald Trump	47
Hillary Clinton	30
Gary Johnson	16
Jill Stein	3

edison
research

Source: NEP Exit Poll conducted by Edison Research

The story gets even more pronounced when we look at the states that swung the election to Trump. In each of the cases in the table below, the votes gained by people who said: "I don't like Trump but I'm going to vote for him anyhow" is greater than his total margin in these states. In other words – it was the "Neithers" who pushed Trump over the top in these states and ultimately won him the election.

State	% "Neithers"	Trump	Clinton
Wisconsin	22%	60%	23%
Pennsylvania	17%	56%	31%
Michigan	20%	50%	29%
Florida	14%	61%	24%
North Carolina	16%	62%	26%

The "Neithers" are more likely to be men (61%) and are more likely to be age 30-44 than in the younger or older age groups. They are 78% white, as compared to the total electorate which is 70%.

One of the most intriguing aspects of the "Neithers" is that a significant portion of those who were unfavorable to both Clinton and Trump were favorable to President Obama. Nearly half of those who didn't like either of this year's two major candidates do have a favorable impression of President Obama – and a significant portion of this group voted for Trump.

The 2016 election was unique in so many ways. One distinguishing characteristic is just how many people had an unfavorable impression of both of the major party candidates. To be sure, some of these people decided not to vote for either – Gary Johnson and Jill Stein combined for 19% of the vote among the "Neithers." However in the end, far more people who liked neither candidate chose Donald Trump and that provided him with his margin of victory in the battleground states.

An analysis of the voting:

It appears there were more people voting against Hillary Clinton than there were voting against Donald Trump.

When sorted by gender: **Male** voters: 53% Trump, 41% Clinton

Female voters: 42% Trump, 54% Clinton

Since there were more female voters than male, (52% vs.48%), Clinton won the popular vote handily. Total vote count: 48.3% for Clinton, 47.28 for Trump.

When sorted by age, an interesting statistic emerges. Age is directly proportional to votes for Trump, and inversely proportional to votes for Clinton. As age increased, more voters favored Trump, 35% of 18 year old voters to 53% of those 65 and over. Conversely, Clinton received 56% from 18 year old voters, but only 45% of those 65 or over. The problem for Clinton, 64% of voters were in the age group of 40 years or older.

The racial divide between Democratic and Republican voters was clear with Trump receiving 58% of white voters, but only 8% of the black vote. Clinton, while getting 88% of the black vote, received only 37% of the white vote. Again, the problem for Clinton, only 12% of the turnout was black, while 70% were white. Clinton also won 65% of Spanish and Asian voters, but their votes only amounted to 15% of the turnout.

Although Clinton won the popular vote by 2,868,691 votes, she lost the Electoral College vote by 74 votes. The problem for Clinton of course, is her votes were not well distributed among the states with the most Electoral College delegates. This is how the Trump campaign staff manipulated the vote by targeting voters from data collected by their internet trolling. They managed to sway just enough voters in those "swing" states to win the Electoral College. In Michigan, 9,528 vote margin out of 4,794,326 votes cast, or .19% - less than one vote for every 500 votes cast! It becomes clear when considering these statistics, how Trump's campaign team was able to secure the election for him by concentrating their efforts on a very small segment of voters which they had identified by their "psychographs".

Selective marketing technology was the obvious winner in this election.

The following article by Gillian Tett illustrates how voters were manipulated.*

*from The Financial Times; reprinted with permission

*"**Why did Donald Trump win?** In recent months we have been offered both sociological and economic answers. But here is another explanation to ponder: computer science. Yes, you read that right. President Trump has never seemed someone who likes to embrace an algorithm. Last year he insisted that he used his "gut" to campaign, since big data were "overrated". That seemed a stark contrast to Hillary Clinton, whose team brimmed with Silicon Valley geeks. Indeed, Clinton campaigners fervently believed they had Big Data on their side, since they had enormous voter lists and all the tech know-how that propelled Barack Obama to victory in 2008. But, like almost everything else in the politics of 2016, appearances were deceptive. Behind the scenes, Mr Trump's aides used data in an innovative way. It raises unsettling questions and also throws down a gauntlet to the corporate world. The issue revolves around a company called Cambridge Analytica, created by British data scientists (the Financial Times has previously used its services in a non-editorial context) and which is now mostly owned by the Mercer family, who are big Republican donors. CA has built a franchise*

by promoting a proprietary technique known as "psychographs," which tries to influence consumers, and voters, with micro-targeted messages designed around market data and psychological profiling. This psychology component comes from a database that the company has created by persuading an astonishingly large number of people to complete surveys on platforms such as Facebook. CA compares this with information it harvests about aspects of those consumers' lives to ascertain psychological patterns. The idea is that if someone knows how you shop, live, communicate, travel and so on, you can extrapolate backwards to create messages that resonate in a psychological sense. "We have a massive database of 4-5,000 data points on every adult in America," Alexander Nix, CA's chief executive, cheerily told me. This sounds weird, if not creepy. Indeed, when I first encountered CA a year ago, I initially wondered if they were cranks. But CA has built a business serving commercial and political clients. Mr Nix says that CA worked for 50 campaigns in America in 2016, all of them Republican (in addition to the Mercer investment, Stephen Bannon, now Mr Trump's chief strategist, has been on the CA board.) The company also advised the Leave campaign in its successful bid to persuade the UK to vote to leave the EU. America Mexican president scraps Trump summit over border wall dispute Enrique Peña Nieto insists his country will not pay for US leader's project The Trump campaign was not always a CA client; initially it worked for his rival

Ted Cruz. But last summer Jared Kushner, Mr Trump's son-in-law, quietly created a data science and campaign group in San Antonio, Texas, modelled like a start-up, and hired CA. While Mr Nix says CA did not have enough time to roll out all its "psychographic" tricks, it used its data to identify which voters could be "flipped" to support Mr Trump, and which Clinton supporters could be persuaded to stay at home with personally targeted messages. They advised Mr Trump on which cities to visit and which messages to use. While the Clinton team used Big Data, they relied more on demographic and polling information of the sort used in 2008. Mr Nix claims that his new technique gave the Trump campaign team a much better "read" of voters, particularly in the crucial swing states just before the vote. It is impossible to prove or disprove these claims, since "psychographs" is a black box. Some Clinton strategists dismiss this tale and point out that a day before the vote CA told reporters (including the FT) that Mrs Clinton would probably win. Other pollsters, such as Frank Luntz, argue that CA were the only data scientists who read voters correctly and "figured out how to win." But if Mr Nix is even partly correct, this raises three points. First, it shows that the noise around Mr Trump does not always match reality. Second, it shows how data science is changing digital privacy and democracy in ways most people do not understand. But third, this story should challenge corporate leaders. There are lots of companies which, like the Clinton team, think they are *unbeatable because of past technological success. But technology can change, and nimble, fast-moving start ups can win in surprising ways. As company executives watch Mr Trump to see what he might do next, they should ponder what he (or, more accurately, Mr Kushner) has already done. It is unsettling — for incumbents of all stripes."*

So there you have it; the explanation of Trump's victory. What happens next? The answer to that question lies in the sentiment and determination of the citizenry. If the emotional response to the Trump victory wanes, our country could see dramatic change in the way our government is perceived around the world and by the American people, and not in a good way. If emotions remain high and the "silent majority" of Americans remains involved in the political process, the result could be to finally return our government to its constituents. The future will be determined either by passivism or activism.

If the fervor created by Trump eventually results in a complete overhaul of our political system, it will prove to be well worth the effort. This will only be accomplished with an aroused citizenry the likes of which hasn't been seen since the early years on our Republic. We are in uncharted territory of immigrant persecution and demagoguery. Does Congress have the backbone to stand up to the President and thwart his efforts on policies which are clearly against everything our nation has stood for? If not, we will be entering the "Dark Age" of American history.

The Aftermath

Turmoil:

The rhetoric from Trump during the campaign and since taking office has emboldened the hate mongers, creating an atmosphere of fear among immigrants from Mexico, the Jewish community and most noticeably Muslims.

During his campaign, Trump proposed the mass deportation of illegal immigrants as part of his immigration policy. Immigration and customs enforcement (ICE) agents have been accused of heartless and brutal treatment of subjects during arrest raids. Taking a cue from Trump they are operating more like the 'Gestapo' than agents of the United States Government.

On March 17th, California Chief Justice asked ICE to stop "stalking" courthouses for the purpose of arresting immigrants. In a letter to U.S. Attorney General Jeff Sessions and John Kelly, Homeland Security Secretary, the Chief Justice said "Courthouses should not be used as bait in the enforcement of immigration laws". "It compromises our core value of fairness and undermines the judiciary's ability to provide equal access to justice."

On February 8, 2017, ICE agents arrested 36-year-old Guadalupe García de Rayos, when she attended her required annual review at the ICE office in Phoenix, and deported her to Mexico the next day based on a removal order issued in 2013. The arrest prompted protests from her family and a small army of volunteers from an immigrants' rights group. She is one of the first to be deported after Trumps crackdown and her deportation reflects the severity of the purge of illegal immigrants. In 2008, she was convicted of possessing a false Social Security number. As a result, she was required to have an annual ICE review to which she voluntarily complied, but when she reported to the ICE office this year, she was arrested and deported.

Trump's order lists reasons for deportation and ends with the phrase; *"or in the judgment of an immigration officer, otherwise pose a risk to public safety or national security."* This wording gives border agents 'free rein' to exceed their authority.

Trump's bigotry has encouraged radicals in our society to act out their hatred in ways not seen in recent memory. Hate crimes against Jews and Muslims have spiked according to FBI records, with a 67% increase in crimes against Muslims in the past year.

"I was a Muslim in Trump's White House"

When President Obama left, I stayed on at the Security Council in order to serve my country.

I lasted eight days.

This article by Rumana Ahmed paints a vivid picture of how the "Trump Effect" has invaded our culture. It is vivid testimony of how Trump's racialism has invaded every level of our society including the White House.

"In 2011, I was hired, straight out of college, to work at the White House and eventually the National Security Council. My job there was to promote and protect the best of what my country stands for. I am a hijab-wearing Muslim woman—I was the only hijabi in the West Wing—

and the Obama administration always made me feel welcome and included.

Like most of my fellow American Muslims, I spent much of 2016 watching with consternation as Donald Trump vilified our community. Despite this––or because of it––I thought I should try to stay on the NSC staff during the Trump Administration, in order to give the new president and his aides a more nuanced view of Islam, and of America's Muslim citizens.

I lasted eight days.

When Trump issued a ban on travelers from seven Muslim-majority countries and all Syrian refugees, I knew I could no longer stay and work for an administration that saw me and people like me not as fellow citizens, but as a threat.

The evening before I left, bidding farewell to some of my colleagues, many of whom have also since left, I notified Trump's senior NSC communications adviser, Michael Anton, of my departure, since we shared an office. His initial surprise, asking whether I was leaving government entirely, was followed by silence—almost in caution, not asking why. I told him anyway.

I told him I had to leave because it was an insult walking into this country's most historic building every day under an administration that is working against and vilifying everything I stand for as an American and as a Muslim. I told him that the administration was attacking the basic tenets of democracy. I told him that I hoped that they and those in Congress were prepared to take responsibility for all the consequences that would attend their decisions.

He looked at me and said nothing.

It was only later that I learned he authored an essay under a pseudonym, extolling the virtues of authoritarianism and attacking diversity as a "weakness," and Islam as "incompatible with the modern West."

My whole life and everything I have learned proves that facile statement wrong.

My parents immigrated to the United States from Bangladesh in 1978 and strove to create opportunities for their children born in the states. My mother worked as a cashier, later starting her own daycare business. My father spent late nights working at Bank of America, and was eventually promoted to assistant vice president at one of its headquarters. Living the American dream, we'd have family barbecues, trips to Disney World, impromptu soccer or football games, and community service projects. My father began pursuing his Ph.D., but in 1995 he was killed in a car accident.

I was 12 when I started wearing a hijab. It was encouraged in my family, but it was always my choice. It was a matter of faith, identity, and resilience for me. After 9/11, everything would change. On top of my shock, horror, and heartbreak, I had to deal with the fear some kids suddenly felt towards me. I was glared at, cursed at, and spat at in public and in school. People called me a "terrorist" and told me, "go back to your country."

My father taught me a Bengali proverb inspired by Islamic scripture: "When a man kicks you down, get back up, extend your hand, and call him brother." Peace, patience, persistence, respect, forgiveness, and dignity. These were the values I've carried through my life and my career.

I never intended to work in government. I was among those who assumed the government was inherently corrupt and ineffective. Working in the Obama White House proved me wrong. You can't know or understand what you haven't been a part of.

Still, inspired by President Obama, I joined the White House in 2011, after graduating from the George Washington University. I had interned there during my junior year, reading letters and taking calls from constituents at the Office of Presidential Correspondence. It felt surreal—here I was, a 22-year-old American Muslim woman from Maryland who had been mocked and called names for covering my hair, working for the president of the United States.

In 2012, I moved to the West Wing to join the Office of Public Engagement, where I worked with various communities, including American Muslims, on domestic issues such as health care. In early 2014, Deputy National Security Advisor Ben Rhodes offered me a position on the National Security Council (NSC). For two and a half years I worked down the hall from the Situation Room, advising President Obama's engagements with American Muslims, and working on issues ranging from advancing relations with Cuba and Laos to promoting global entrepreneurship among women and youth.

A harsher world began to reemerge in 2015. In February, three young American Muslim students were killed in their Chapel Hill home by an Islamophobe. Both the media and administration were slow to address the attack, as if the dead had to be vetted before they could be mourned. It was emotionally devastating. But when a statement was finally released condemning the attack and mourning their loss, Rhodes took me aside to tell me how grateful he was to have me there and wished there were more American Muslims working throughout government. America's government and decision-making should reflect its people.

Later that month, the evangelist Franklin Graham declared that the government had "been infiltrated by Muslims." One of my colleagues sought me out with a smile on his face and said, "If only he knew they were in the halls of the West Wing and briefed the president of the United States multiple times!" I thought: Damn right I'm here, exactly where I belong, a proud American dedicated to protecting and serving my country.

Graham's hateful provocations weren't new. Over the Obama years, right-wing websites spread an abundance of absurd conspiracy theories and lies, targeting some American Muslim organizations and individuals——even those of us serving in government. They called us "terrorists," Sharia-law whisperers, or Muslim Brotherhood operatives. Little did I realize that some of these conspiracy theorists would someday end up in the White House.

Over the course of the campaign, even when I was able to storm through the bad days, I realized the rhetoric was taking a toll on American communities. When Trump first called for a Muslim ban, reports of hate crimes against Muslims spiked. The trend of anti-Muslim hate crimes is ongoing, as mosques are set on fire and individuals attacked—six were killed at a mosque in Canada by a self-identified Trump supporter.

Throughout 2015 and 2016, I watched with disbelief, apprehension, and anxiety, as Trump's style of campaigning instigated fear and emboldened xenophobes, anti-Semites, and Islamophobes. While cognizant of the possibility of Trump winning, I hoped a majority of the electorate would never condone such a hateful and divisive worldview.

During the campaign last February, Obama visited a Baltimore mosque and reminded the public that "we're one American family, and when any part of our family starts to feel separate ... It's a challenge to our values." His words would go unheeded by his successor.

The climate in 2016 felt like it did just after 9/11. What made it worse was that this fear and hatred were being fueled by Americans in positions of power. Fifth-grade students at a local Sunday school where I volunteered shared stories of being bullied by classmates and teachers, feeling like they didn't belong here anymore, and asked if they might get kicked out of this country if Trump won. I was almost hit by a car by a white man laughing as he drove by in a Costco parking lot, and on another occasion was followed out of the metro by a man screaming profanities: "Fuck you! Fuck Islam! Trump will send you back!"

While cognizant of the possibility of Trump winning, I hoped a majority of the electorate would never condone such a hateful and divisive worldview.

Then, on election night, I was left in shock.

The morning after the election, we lined up in the West Colonnade as Obama stood in the Rose Garden and called for national unity and a smooth transition. Trump seemed the antithesis of everything we stood for. I felt lost. I could not fully grasp the idea that he would soon be sitting where Obama sat.

I debated whether I should leave my job. Since I was not a political appointee, but a direct hire of the NSC, I had the option to stay. The incoming and now departed national security adviser, Michael Flynn, had said things like "fear of Muslims is rational." Some colleagues and community leaders encouraged me to stay, while others expressed concern for my safety. Cautiously optimistic, and feeling a responsibility to try to help them continue our work and be heard, I decided that Trump's NSC could benefit from a colored, female, hijab-wearing, American Muslim patriot.

The weeks leading up to the inauguration prepared me and my colleagues for what we thought would come, but not for what actually came. On Monday, January 23, I walked into the Eisenhower Executive Office Building, with the new staffers there. Rather than the excitement I encountered when I first came to the White House under Obama, the new staff looked at me with a cold surprise. The diverse White House I had worked in became a monochromatic and male bastion.

The days I spent in the Trump White House were strange, appalling and disturbing. As one staffer serving since the Reagan administration said, "This place has been turned upside down. It's chaos. I've never witnessed anything like it." This was not typical Republican leadership, or even that of a businessman. It was a chaotic attempt at authoritarianism—legally questionable executive orders, accusations of the press being "fake," peddling countless lies as "alternative facts," and assertions by White House surrogates that the president's national security authority would "not be questioned."

The entire presidential support structure of nonpartisan national security and legal experts within the White House complex and across federal agencies was being undermined. Decision-making authority was now centralized to a few in the West Wing. Frustration and mistrust developed as some staff felt out of the loop on issues within their purview. There was no structure or clear guidance. Hallways were eerily quiet as key positions and offices responsible for national security or engagement with Americans were left unfilled.

Placing U.S. national security in the hands of people who think America's diversity is a "weakness" is dangerous.

I might have lasted a little longer. Then came January 30. The executive order banning travelers from seven Muslim-majority countries caused chaos, without making America any safer. Discrimination that has existed for years at airports was now legitimized, sparking mass protests, while the president railed against the courts for halting his ban. Not only was this discrimination and un-American, the administration's actions defending the ban threatened the nation's security and its system of checks and balances.

Alt-right writers, now on the White House staff, have claimed that Islam and the West are at war with each other. Disturbingly, ISIS also makes such claims to justify their attacks, which for the most part target Muslims. The Administration's plans to revamp the Countering Violent Extremism program to focus solely on Muslims and use terms like "radical Islamic terror," legitimize ISIS propaganda and allow the dangerous rise of white-supremacist extremism to go unchecked.

Placing U.S. national security in the hands of people who think America's diversity is a "weakness" is dangerous. It is false.

People of every religion, race, ethnicity, sexual orientation, gender, and age pouring into the streets and airports to defend the rights of their fellow Americans over the past few weeks proved the opposite is true— American diversity is a strength, and so is the American commitment to ideals of justice and equality.

American history is not without stumbles, which have proven that the nation is only made more prosperous and resilient through struggle, compassion and inclusiveness. It's why my parents came here. It's why I told my former 5th grade students, who wondered if they still belonged here, that this country would not be great without them."
*End of article

It is a travesty of our American heritage and everything we stand for as a nation to tolerate the dismantling of the freedom and values that have been so dearly won since the creation of this great nation. Yes, let us make America great again, not in the image of Mr. Trump, but an America of inclusiveness, compassion and freedom to pursue ones' dreams. Let us stand up for humanity. We cannot let our entire system fail because of one man.

Trump has done nothing to allay the fears that accompanied his election, just one week after the inauguration he issued this travel ban against immigration from seven majority Muslin countries which took effect immediately, creating havoc for immigrants arriving at airports across the country.

Executive Order 13769:

"Protecting the Nation from Foreign Terrorist Entry into the United States",
January 27, 2017.

Over a hundred travelers were detained and held for hours without access to family or legal assistance. In addition, up to 60,000 visas were "provisionally revoked", according to the State Department. Within hours lawsuits were filed arguing that the order, or actions taken pursuant to the order, violated the U.S. Constitution, federal statutes, and treaty obligations. Federal courts issued emergency orders halting detention, expulsion, or blocking of lawful travelers, pending final rulings.

Domestically, the order was criticized by Democratic and Republican members of Congress, universities, business leaders, Catholic bishops, and Jewish organizations. A record 1,000 U.S. diplomats signed a cable opposing the order. Protests erupted in airports and cities. Internationally, the order prompted broad condemnation, including from longstanding U.S. allies. The travel ban and suspension of refugee admissions was criticized by top UN officials and by a group of 40 Nobel laureates and thousands of other academics

Many were held in detention at the airports and sent back from whence they came. Indignation was widespread and demonstrations at airports sprang up in support of those being detained and refused entry. A day after the order went into effect, a federal judge in Brooklyn issued an emergency stay to stop deportation of those caught in the ban and ordering release of travelers with valid visas who were being held at U.S. airports. The next day, the new Homeland security secretary issued a waiver excluding lawful permanent residents from the ban. The following day, Washington state attorney general sues the Trump administration asking for a temporary restraining order blocking the ban. Two days later, four additional states sue Trump over the ban. February 3rd, one week after the executive order, a Washington state district court judge issues a restraining order suspending the ban nationwide.

The degree of harm to our relationship with the nations of the world due to this hasty and ill advised executive order is difficult to measure, but is undoubtedly substantial. Immigrants that had worked for months or years to obtain visas to immigrate were told they could not board their flight to the U.S., or they were sent back after arrival in our country.

Time line of events:

January 27th, Travel ban issued

January 28th, Federal judge issues an emergency stay.

January 29th, Washington State A.G. sues the administration asking for restraining order.

January 31st, Four additional states sue Trump re the ban.

February 3rd, Washington State judge issues restraining order suspending the ban.

February 3rd, 6:08 PM
Trump tweet, *"We must keep "evil" out of our country!"*

February 3rd, Travel from the affected countries resumes.

February 4th, 8:12 AM

Trump tweet: "*The opinion of this so-called judge, which essentially takes law-enforcement away from our country, is ridiculous and will be overturned!*"

February 4th, Justice department asks for an emergency ruling to overturn the Washington state decision. Request denied.

February 4th, 3:44 PM
Trump tweet: "*What is our country coming to when a judge can halt a Homeland Security travel ban and anyone, even with bad intentions, can come into U.S.?*"

February 4th, 4:44 PM
Trump tweet: "*Because the ban was lifted by a judge, many very bad and dangerous people may be pouring into our country. A terrible decision*"

February 5th, 3:39 PM
Trump tweet: "*Just cannot believe a judge would put our country in such peril. If something happens blame him and court system. People pouring in. Bad!*"

February 7th, Appeals court hears arguments by lawyers for the government and Washington state.

February 8th, 7:03 AM
Trump Tweet: *"If the U.S. does not win this case as it so obviously should, we can never have the security and safety to which we are entitled. Politics!"*

February 9th, The appeals court declines to block Washington states' restraining order saying the government provided no evidence of a threat from travelers from the affected countries. Following the decision:

February 9th, 6:35 PM
Trump Tweet: *"SEE YOU IN COURT, THE SECURITY OF OUR NATION IS AT STAKE!"*

Is this Presidential behavior, or more that of a petulant child? Trump's disdain for the judicial branch of the Government causes a great deal of concern. It is the Judiciary that defends our Constitution and limits overreaching by the Congress or the President.

In response to Trump's comments, Judge Jay Bybee and four other judges from the U.S. Court of Appeals for the 9th Circuit, replied: *"I have the greatest respect for my colleagues. The personal attacks on the distinguished district judge and our colleagues were out of bounds of civic and persuasive discourse – particularly when they came from the parties.(the President).* "It does no credit to the arguments of the parties to impugn the motives or the competence of the members of this court; ad hominem attacks are not a substitute for effective advocacy. Such personal attacks treat the court as though it were merely a political forum in which bargaining, compromise and even intimidation are acceptable principles. The courts of law must be more than that, or we are not governed by law at all."*

Temporarily finished with attacking the judicial system, Trump turned his attention to the News Media.   On 2/17, he began a series of Tweets belittling most of the national news outlets.

February 17th, 1:48 PM

Trump Tweet: "The FAKE NEWS media (failing @nytimes, @NBCNews, @ABC, @CBS, @CNN) is not my enemy, it is the enemy of the American People!"

That tweet followed up a previous tweet that he deleted, in which he made a nearly identical attack.

February 17th, 4:32 PM

Trump Tweet: "The FAKE NEWS media (failing @nytimes, @CNN, @NBCNews and many more) is not my enemy, it is the enemy of the American people," he wrote. "SICK!"

Trump posted his fix to the original tweet 16 minutes later, replacing "SICK!" with the names of two additional news outlets, ABC and CBS.

February 17th, 4:48 PM

Trump Tweet: "The FAKE NEWS media (failing @nytimes, @NBCNews, @ABC, @CBS, @CNN) is not my enemy, it is the enemy of the American People!

The President has attempted to discredit a wide range of negative reporting on his administration as "fake news" and "very fake news."

Trump's tweets usually follow a TV news report.

Fox News "O'Reilly Factor" on crime in Chicago, followed by Trump tweet:

"I will send in the Feds".

"Fox and Friends" report of violence at U. of C. Berkley followed by Trump tweet:

"NO FEDERAL FUNDS".

"Fox and Friends" report Russia "ran right over" Obama for eight years, followed by Trump tweet:

"For eight years Russia "ran over" President Obama".

Is this life imitating art? This isn't SNL, it's real.

It would be comical were it not so frightening!

Made for TV:

On February 28th President Trump made his first speech to the joint members of Congress. It was an attempt at damage control after a disastrous 40 days in office. He outlined his goals for legislation: a huge increase in Defense spending, removing environmental protections which inhibit industry and coal mining, a push for completion of the Keystone and Dakota Access Pipelines, removing the United States from the Trans-Pacific Partnership, increasing immigration enforcement, building the stupid wall, reducing corporate and personal income taxes, increasing import taxes, imposing educational and income requirements for immigration, rebuilding our national infrastructure, repealing and replacing Obamacare.

Trump's showmanship was on full display. He introduced Denisha Merriweather, a student who had struggled in grade school but was helped by tax credits and scholarships and has now graduated from college. He also introduced the father of Jamiel Shaw Jr. who was murdered by an illegal immigrant. He then called attention to Susan Oliver and Jessica Davis in the balcony with Susan's daughter Jenna. Deputy Sheriff Danny Oliver and Detective Michael Davis were also slain by an illegal immigrant. He stated he had ordered the Department of Homeland Security to create an office to serve victims of Immigration crime.

The highlight of his speech he saved for last, a tribute to Ryan Owens, the Navy Seal who lost his life in the ill fated raid on al Qaeda. While speaking of Ryan, the cameras panned to his widow seated in the gallery. She was sobbing as Trump praised her dead husband. It was an obvious attempt by Trump to capitalize on the sentimental moment to show his compassion. It is unfortunate that Ryan's widow had to be a pawn in the process. It is commendable that Ryan's father did not attend this staging. He had earlier in the month refused to meet with Trump when the President visited the family and this speaks volumes for his integrity. As much as he wanted to see his son honored for his sacrifice, he did not want to legitimize Trump's motives.

Trumped Up?

Trump tweet "crosses the line":

Early on a Saturday morning, March 4th, Trump set off a firestorm with an outrageous tweet at 6:35 AM accusing former President Obama of having his phone wiretapped. If, in fact, it were true, it would be the first time a sitting President accused his predecessor of a crime. Offering no evidence to support the allegations, lawmakers are waiting for proof. In the meantime, it appears to be not only a stupid charge, but "Trumped Up".

March 4th, 6:35AM
"Terrible! Just found out that Obama had my "wires tapped" in Trump Tower just before the victory. Nothing found. This is McCarthyism!"

March 4th, 6:49 PM
"Is it legal for a sitting President to be "wire tapping" a race for president prior to an election? Turned down by court earlier. A NEW LOW!"

March 4th, 6:52 AM
***"I'd bet a good lawyer could make a great case out of the fact that President Obama was tapping my phones in October,** just prior to Election!"*

March 4th, 7:02 AM
"How low has President Obama gone to tapp my phones during the very sacred election process. This is Nixon/Watergate. Bad (or sick) guy!"

Kevin Lewis, Obama's spokesman, said in a statement: "A cardinal rule of the Obama Administration was that no White House official ever interfered with any independent investigation led by the Department of Justice."

"As part of that practice, neither President Obama nor any White House official ever ordered surveillance on any U.S. citizen," he said. "Any suggestion otherwise is simply false."

James Clapper, Director of National Intelligence: "there was no such wiretap activity mounted against the president, the president elect at the time"

Trumps Tweets portray a man that is very impulsive, disturbed and egocentric. Unfortunately, he is also our President.

Our Worst Nightmare:
March 6, 2017: U.S. Strategic Command said North Korea launched four guided missiles from a launch site on North Korea's west coast near the border with China. The missiles flew 600 miles across the country before splashing into the Sea of Japan. In Japan, the government said three of the missiles had landed within 200 miles of their coastline. The most disturbing factor in this exhibition, the Pentagon says North Korea's leader, Kim Jong-Un, is acting more "*irrationally and unpredictably*" than previously.

When you consider two world leaders, half a world apart, sharing similar personality traits, both having the keys to their nuclear arsenals, we must be very afraid for the future of mankind.

Other Trump orders causing consternation:

Executive order 13765: Minimizing the Economic Burden of the Patient Protection and Affordable Care Act Pending Repeal:

This order casts a spell of uncertainty over the administration of the Affordable Care Act and the effort to replace it is creating confusion and animosity among all the players. One thing is certain; the final American Health Care Act will not be popular among most Americans.

*Charles M. Blow, commenting in the NYT opinion section:
"Donald Trump has sold his supporters – and by extension, this country – a ticket to hell."

Executive Order 13767: Border Security and Immigration Enforcement Improvements:

The orders directs "executive departments and agencies to deploy all lawful means to secure the United States' southern border, to prevent further illegal immigration into the United States, and to repatriate illegal aliens swiftly, consistently, and humanely"[1] and directs the Secretary of Homeland Security to "secure the southern Border of the United States of America" using Border Patrol agents and the Attorney General to take measures for prosecution of illegal immigration or other offenses in connection with the southern border.[1]

The order states that construction of a physical wall "or other similarly secure, contiguous, and impassable physical barrier" on the southern border of the United States must immediately be constructed, and that it be monitored by "adequate personnel" to prevent **illegal immigration, drug trafficking and human trafficking**, and acts of terrorism.

Trump has repeatedly vowed that Mexico will pay for construction of a border wall, but has never explained how the U.S. government would compel Mexico to do so. On one occasion, Trump said "There will be a payment; it will be in a form, perhaps a complicated form"—indicating that he might attempt to curtail **U.S. foreign aid** to Mexico.[7] The Mexican government has rejected Trump's statements.[7] Upon signing the order, the Trump administration also suggested that wall construction could be funded by a 20% tariff on Mexico imports, a proposal which immediately encountered objections from members of Congress of both parties.

U.S. Representative **Michael McCaul**, Republican of Austin, Texas, the chairman of the **House Homeland Security Committee**, said that the Republican-controlled **U.S. House of Representatives** would seek to pass a special **supplemental appropriations bill** to spend money on initial construction of the wall. McCaul is supported by **House Speaker Paul Ryan.**

The executive order has made relations with the U.S. and Mexico very difficult. **Mexican President Enrique Peña Nieto** condemned Trump's executive order and again said that Mexico would not pay for the wall's construction.

Addressing supporters, the Mexican opposition leader **Andrés Manuel López Obrador** condemned the wall order as an insult to **Mexico.**

There are doubts about whether a wall would actually stem illegal immigration, or if it is worth the billions it is expected to cost, considering that the number of illegal immigrants in the U.S. has declined for the past several years.

The rugged terrain in the Arizona desert is one of many natural obstacles in the construction of the wall. There is currently 700 miles of fencing, and the border is patrolled by agents using motorcycles, ATVs and **drone surveillance.**

Trump's order is dangerous for the immediate and long-term security and economy of the United States.

Mexico will not, as Trump promised during the campaign; pay for the useless wall along the border. So his spokesman, Sean Spicer, **stated** that a border tax on Mexican products would, in fact, pay for the wall. As economists quickly pointed out, however, tariffs aren't paid by the exporter. A tariff on Mexican goods would be a tax on U.S. consumers. America, not Mexico, would end up paying for the wall.

Executive Order 13772: *"Core Principles for Regulating the United States Financial System":*

Establishes the "core principles" of regulation under the Trump Administration places under review the Dodd–Frank Wall Street Reform and Consumer Protection Act.

Dodd-Frank was designed to protect consumers from abusive financial services practices and to protect American taxpayers from paying for bailouts. It was also designed to promote financial stability by improving accountability and transparency on Wall Street.

Repealing Dodd-Frank is a good thing?

Rebuild America's Infrastructure:

Executive Order 13766 of January 24, 2017

Section 1. Purpose. Infrastructure investment strengthens our economic platform, makes America more competitive, creates millions of jobs, increases wages for American workers, and reduces the costs of goods and services for American families and consumers. Too often, infrastructure projects in the United States have been routinely and excessively delayed by agency processes and procedures. These delays have increased project costs and blocked the American people from the full benefits of increased infrastructure investments, which are important to allowing Americans to compete and win on the world economic stage. Federal infrastructure decisions should be accomplished with maximum efficiency and effectiveness, while also respecting property rights and protecting public safety and the environment. To that end, it is the policy of the executive branch to streamline and expedite, in a manner consistent with law, environmental reviews and approvals for all infrastructure projects, especially projects that are a high priority for the Nation, such as improving the U.S. electric grid and telecommunications systems and repairing and upgrading critical port facilities, airports, pipelines, bridges, and highways.

Again, nothing in the form of a specific plan has been proposed by the administration and it will depend on the cooperation of Congress to formulate and agree to a plan.

Greenlight pipelines like DAPL and Keystone

January 24, 2017

Presidential Memorandum Regarding Construction of the Keystone XL Pipeline

Section 1. Policy. In accordance with Executive Order 11423 of August 16, 1968, as amended, and Executive Order 13337 of April 30, 2004, the Secretary of State has delegated authority to receive applications for Presidential permits for the construction, connection, operation, or maintenance, at the borders of the United States, of facilities for the exportation or importation of petroleum, petroleum products, coal, or other fuels to or from a foreign country, and to issue or deny such Presidential permits.

As set forth in those Executive Orders, the Secretary of State should issue a Presidential permit for any cross-border pipeline project that "would serve the national interest."

As promised, the President is going ahead with the Keystone Pipeline against the objections of environmentalists who claim the increase of oil production from the Canadian oil sands create 15 percent more greenhouse gas emissions than the average method for crude production used in the United States. It is predicted that if all the oil in the Canadian sands was extracted, the effect would be a permanent degradation of the U.S. climate.

Presidential Memorandum Regarding Construction of the Dakota Access Pipeline:

January 24, 2017

MEMORANDUM FOR THE SECRETARY OF THE ARMY

SUBJECT: Construction of the Dakota Access Pipeline

Section 1. Policy. The Dakota Access Pipeline (DAPL) under development by Dakota Access, LLC, represents a substantial, multi-billion-dollar private investment in our Nation's energy infrastructure. This approximately 1,100-mile pipeline is designed to carry approximately 500,000 barrels per day of crude oil from the Bakken and Three Forks oil production areas in North Dakota to oil markets in the United States. At this time, the DAPL is more than 90 percent complete across its entire route. Only a limited portion remains to be constructed.

The rub here, of course, is the Standing Rock Sioux Tribe who claim the project would contaminate drinking water and damage sacred burial sites. The Sioux claim

the land was taken from them illegally in an 1868 treaty. Reactivating the project will certainly create another unfortunate standoff between the Sioux and the U.S. Government.

Reverse environment restrictions:
January 24, 2017

SUBJECT: Streamlining Permitting and Reducing Regulatory Burdens for Domestic Manufacturing

Section 1. Purpose. This memorandum directs executive departments and agencies (agencies) to support the expansion of manufacturing in the United States through expedited reviews of and approvals for proposals to construct or expand manufacturing facilities and through reductions in regulatory burdens affecting domestic manufacturing.

Good for business, bad for everyone else. After years of battling to obtain reasonable guidelines for protecting the environment from the ravages of American manufacturing plants, this regulatory directive will essentially put us back at square one.

Trump signs order to dismantle environment protections.
Presidential Executive Order on Promoting Energy Independence and Economic Growth
March 28, 2017

Revokes:
1. Exec. Order 13653 of 11/1/2013: preparing the United States for the impacts of Climate Change.
2. Presidential Memorandum of 6/25/2013: Power Sector

Carbon Pollution Standards.
3. Presidential Memorandum of 11/3/2015: Mitigating impacts on Natural Resources from Development and Encouraging Related Private Investment.
4. Presidential Memorandum of 9/21/2016: Climate Change and National Security.

Recinds:

1. Report of the President of 6/2013: The President's Climate Action Plan.
2. Report of the President of 3/2014: Climate Action Plan Strategy to Reduce Methane Emissions.

Trump has "Sold our soul to the Devil". Sacrificing

hard won environmental gains to satisfy his agenda, ignorant of the consequences to our citizens' health and to our country. There is seemingly no limit to the brash, poorly thought out and executed orders emanating from the White House. The damage this man could do in just a few years as President is frightening!

3/9/2017: Trump's EPA Administrator, Scott Pruitt speaking on CNBC's "Squawk Box", said "Carbon Dioxide is *not* a primary contributor to climate change". This is the man Trump put in charge of protecting our environment, and he doesn't believe in the # 1 cause of global warming?

NASA and the NOAA stated that last year's record warm temperatures were "driven largely by increased carbon dioxide and other human-made emissions in the atmosphere"

The EPA, the agency responsible for protecting our environment, and the one Mr. Pruitt heads, states the "primary greenhouse gas that is contributing to recent climate change, is carbon dioxide".

Trump and his minions are trying to take apart the progress made in protecting our environment brick by brick.

Resistance:

The day after the inauguration, millions of people joined together, marching in solidarity against the man who was sworn in as our 45th President and the policies of his new administration. According to crowd scientists, 470,000 people filled the streets in Washington, D.C. at or near the mall – roughly three times the number which had attended the inauguration the day before. Crowds filled the streets in cities across the country from Boston to Los Angeles, from Minneapolis to Austin, totaling 4.2 million according to crowd size specialist of the University of Denver, making it the largest single day demonstration in U.S. history.

Throughout the day, President Trump ignored what these millions of demonstrators were saying; we will not go away quietly, we will not be forced into submission, we will speak up for our rights.

When Trumps ill-conceived travel ban began creating havoc for travelers, thousands of demonstrators poured into the nations' airports to protest. Employees at Silicon Valley tech firms left their jobs to join in and show their anger. An outpouring of citizens from all walks of life joined together to register their dismay with the Presidents' precipitous actions. Lawyers came to the airports as soon as news filtered out concerning the dire conditions and filed emergency briefs in attempts to obtain a stay in the execution of the Presidents' order. In just a few days, President Trump had managed to create a huge amount of angst for Americans.

The Chinese Consulate warned "Chinese exchange students, visiting students, teachers and volunteers" to avoid participating in the protests.

Turkey warned its' citizens who may be traveling to the United States to "be careful due to protests" and stated that "racist and xenophobic incidents increased in the USA".

Protests were not limited to the United States. Canada, France, Germany, Australia, U.K., Philippines and Israel all had huge demonstrations against Trump

Protesters marched on Trumps' Mar-a-Lago resort in Florida. New York City saw thousands gather at the historic Stonewall Inn. In San Francisco, thousands rallied against Trump outside the San Francisco City Hall. Three weeks after Trump was sworn in, thousands joined together on Ocean Beach in San Francisco to spell out the word "RESIST". Anti-Trump rallies were held in Edinburgh, Scotland, Prague, Czech Republic and Raleigh, North Carolina.

In Mexico City, 20,000 people marched in protest of Trumps policies on immigration. Other Mexican cities holding protest marches included Monterrey, Morelia, Merida and Tijuana.

Obviously, there are a lot of people around the globe that see President Trump as a menace.

The acrimony directed toward our country since Trump took office is evident even from our traditional allies. His behavior will make it difficult to reconstruct relationships with world powers due to his impetuous actions based on faulty evidence and his questionable relationship with the truth.

Adam Schiff of California, member of the House Intelligence Committee, stated:

"We must accept the possibility that @POTUS does not know fact from fiction, right from wrong. That wild claims are not strategic, but worse."

"The implications are quite extraordinary, how much credibility will the president have left to persuade the country of what has happened, what needs to be done? How much credibility will he have with our

allies to get them to back us up? So these have real-world repercussions – It's the president losing the credibility of the office."

When public statements of this nature are made by a respected member of Congress about our President, it underscores the need for a real person in the White House.

Trump's "Foot in Mouth" disease resulted in having his second, revamped Muslin Ban rejected by the courts. On March 6th, a new "improved" version of the January 27th ban was signed by the President to take effect on March 15th, and the day before it was to become effective, a federal judge in Hawaii issued a nationwide stay order blocking implementation of the executive order. The reasoning of the court relied heavily on comments made by Trump on the campaign trail and since taking office. *"The record before this Court is unique. It includes significant and un-rebutted evidence of religious animus driving the promulgation of the Executive Order and its related predecessor."*

Trump actions which are cause for alarm:

3/6/17 New 6 country travel ban

2/28/17 Revision of the "Clean Water Rule"

2/24/17 Enforcing Regulatory Reform

2/3/17 Reviewing Wall Street Regulations

2/3/17 Reviewing the Fiduciary Duty Rule

1/28/17 Reorganizing the National and Homeland Security Council; (Puts Steve Bannon on the NSC)

1/28/17 School Choice Week

1/27/17 First Immigration Ban

1/27/17 "Rebuild the Military"

1/25/17 Border Security and Immigration enforcement

1/25/17 Stops Funding for Sanctuary Cities

1/24/17 Approves Keystone XL and Dakota Access Pipeline

1/24/17 Reduce regulations for U.S. Manufacturers

1/23/17 Reinstates "Mexico City Policy"

1/23/17 Withdraws from Trans Pacific Partnership

1/20/17 Repeal Affordable Care Act

Troublesome Cabinet Appointments:

EPA: Scott Pruitt, who has been quoted as saying "The debate is far from settled" over whether human activity has contributed to the warming of the earth. This is the man in charge of protecting our environment?

Dept of Energy: Rick Perry, who said he would eliminate the Energy Department and then forgot he said it. He was also unaware that his department was responsible for managing nuclear waste.

Secretary of Education: Betsy DeVos, generous donor to the Republican Party and strong advocate for Charter Schools and school voucher programs is also a proponent for Common Core.

Secretary of Defense: Gen. James Mattis, known as "Mad Dog", has been quoted as saying "It's fun to shoot some people", seems a perfect fit for Trump.

Attorney General: Jeff Sessions, accused of making racist comments over the years is another perfect fit for Trump.

The Trump Budget:

To call this a disaster is not doing it justice. It defies logic, reason and common sense. He is not only asking for a 54 Billion dollar increase in a military budget that is already twice its proper size, but he is asking to cut every humanitarian function our government performs, and in many cases to eliminate them altogether.

It is imperative for our Congress to take a stand; say enough is enough and reject this budget as completely unacceptable.

Some of the outrageous aspects of this budget:

Increases:

- Military spending by 54 Billion to increase the number of "warfighteers", buy more ships for the Navy and more F- 35 fighter planes for the Air Force.
- Dept. of Homeland Security to pay for "The Wall", 500 new border patrol agents and 1000 new ICE agents.
- Funding for the Dept. of Veterans Affairs.

Decreases:

- Agriculture Dept. staff reductions at USDA, reduces funding for Women, Infants and Children programs and eliminates the McGovern-Dole International Food for Education program.
- Commerce Dept. eliminates Sea Grant University co-op program, cuts funding for Climate-change and ocean research at NOAA.
- Education Dept. cuts 3.7 Billion for teacher training, after school and summer programs, but increases charter school funding.
- Energy Dept. eliminates the Energy Star and Advanced Technology Vehicle Manufacturing Program.
- Health and Human Services Dept. decreases funding for NIH and eliminates partnerships between U.S. and foreign health institutions. "Meals on Wheels" is funded by this department.
- Housing and Urban Development eliminates Block Grant Program, Home investment and self-help Homeownership Opportunity Programs.
- Interior Dept. eliminates funding for the 49 National Historic Sites.

- Justice Dept. reduces federal prison construction and hires more U.S. Marshals and border enforcement prosecutors.
- Labor Dept. reduces funding for job-training programs for seniors and disadvantaged youth.
- State Dept. Eliminates climate-change prevention programs as well as payments pledged to U.N. climate-change programs.
- Transportation Dept. privatizes air traffic control and eliminates funding for new transit programs and for long-distance Amtrak.
- Treasury Dept: eliminates grants for Community Development Financial Institutions.
- Environmental Protection Agency: The EPA eliminates over 50 programs and over 3000 jobs. Discontinues funding for international climate-change programs. Cuts funding for the Office of Enforcement and Compliance and the Superfund cleanup program.
- NASA: Cuts Earth-Observation and education programs, terminating missions to understanding climate-change.
- Small Business Administration: Cuts funding for loan guarantees for small business owners and eliminates Prime technical assistance grants.
- Arts and Humanities: *Completely eliminate* funding for the following:
  - African Development Foundation
  - Appalachian Regional Commission
  - Chemical Safety Board
  - Corporation for National and Community Service
  - Corporation for Public Broadcasting
  - Delta Regional Authority
  - Denali Commission

- Institute of Museum and Library Services
- Inter-American Foundation
- U.S. Trade and Development Agency
- Legal Services Corporation
- National Endowment for the Arts
- National Endowment for the Humanities
- Neighborhood Reinvestment Corporation
- Northern Border Regional Commission
- Overseas Private Investment Corporation
- U.S. Institute of Peace
- U.S. Interagency Council on Homelessness
- Woodrow Wilson International Center for Scholars

To what degree Trump's budget becomes final will depend on how many Republicans in Congress are willing to be "thrown under the bus". There will be a considerable amount of "horse-trading" among congressional members between the Budget and the Tax Bill. The end result, unfortunately, will probably be two disastrous bills.

The Future:

1 Goal: Blunt Trump

Cardinal concepts to fight for:

Humanitarianism
Debt reduction
Military restructure

The challenge: To garner the sentiment against Trump's agenda and blunt his actions by gaining control of Congress. How can this be accomplished? It's not easy, but it is doable.

If Trump continues to be "Trump", voter turnout for change should be substantial.

"Now is the time for all good men to come to the aid of their country".

If you are from an earlier era, and had a typing class in school, you typed this phrase a thousand times. The creator of this phrase undoubtedly had in mind maximum finger dexterity, but it could not be more timely and relevant than today. For now *is* the time for all good men *and women* to come to the aid of their country. Our country is faced with a crisis unparalleled in recent history.

The "Women's March on Washington" illustrated how deeply concerned our citizens are with the Trump administration. Demonstrations in Washington and every major city in the country and around the globe brought out over three million protestors. Comments from participants: Awe-inspiring; Energizing; Mobilizing.

How do persons who were motivated to demonstrate convert those energies into political action?

1. **You need a plan.**
2. **You need people to implement the plan.**
3. **You need to see it through to conclusion.**

The Plan:

Obtain control of Congress in the 2018 elections and the White House in 2020. The mid-term elections in 2018 are crucial to forming a beachhead against the prevailing political structure. Finding candidates, male and female, with the "balls" to fight the establishment will be challenging, but an absolute necessity.

1. Search for an organization whose goals are aligned with yours, attend meetings and enlist friends to join you. Fight for redistricting where needed.
2. Vet potential congressional candidates in regard to their fervor for supporting humanitarianism, a modern military and debt reduction.
3. Enlist candidates who can win elections for congressional seats in 2018 and support their candidacy.
4. Support the independent thinkers on both sides of the aisle.
5. Seek out Republican Congressional members who have aligned themselves against Trump's policies and help them be reelected.

Implement the plan:
Enroll neighbors and internet friends in the cause.

Become active in the local Democratic, Republican or independent organization. The candidate's party affiliation should not be as important as their beliefs. Use the internet to contact and enlist others who are repulsed by the current administration and write daily to your congressional representatives. Whether this will have lasting results will be borne out in the elections of 2018. When the Republicans in Congress see the sentiment among their constituents has become hostile to their actions, they will become more amenable to the new agenda. If there is to be change, it will have to come by making the Congress more aware of their fiduciary duty to the American people. There has been an atmosphere of "us or them" for many years now and it is time to make it more about "we". This can only occur by badgering our representatives in Congress to the extent that they understand they will be replaced if they do not work for the good of the country rather than for the good of their special interests.

Levels of involvement:

1. Identify your members of Congress
2. Use the web to express your feelings or support a cause.
3. Telephone your Congressional Member's Office
4. Join a group of like-minded activists to coordinate actions

Results will occur when hundreds or thousands of tweets or emails are directed to the proper source, but "bodies on the street" is still a necessary requirement to guarantee the attention of our Senators and Representatives.

The ACLU has a "Freedom Cities" campaign that is concentrating on fighting for the fair and humane treatment of immigrants. Organizations like the *ACLU*, *Women4ChangeIndiana.org* and

Count MI Vote.org in Michigan are at the forefront of working to blunt Trump's actions and elect real people to Congress. It is through these "Grass Roots" organizations and others like them that change will come.

Groups that may be helpful:

Indivisibleguide.com	Womensmarch.com
Govtrack.us	CountMiVote.org
Phonecongress.com	MichiganForRevolution.com
Meetup.com	Women4ChangeIndiana.org
Techworkerscoalition.org	Independentvoting.org
Unaffiliatedparty.org	Twitter.com#theresistance
Ivn.us	Change.org
Teaparty.org	MoveOn.org
Asdc.democrates.org	Gop.com

It may seem incongruous to list the website for the Republican Party, but the individual candidate's beliefs should be more important than their party affiliation. Senate Republican Rand Paul is an example of voting one's conscience rather than toeing the party line. We need more independent thinkers on both sides of the aisle.

If there is some "good" to come from Trump's election, it has been the mobilization of citizens who have been silent and passive in the past, but are now motivated to take action.

ACLU: The "Freedom Cities" Campaign: Resistance through Progress at the Local Level. *Excerpt from an article by Ronald Newman

"Freedom Cities encourages and supports grassroots activism aimed at driving policy change at the local level. It allows individuals and groups to come together to actively shape how we treat vulnerable communities, how we cherish and safeguard fundamental freedoms, and how we respond as a society to the needs of our families, friends, and neighbors."

Recent events have catapulted our treatment of immigrants and racial minorities into our national consciousness: Candidates for office should be vetted for their stand on inclusion and humanitarianism. We cannot treat our country as an "island fortress".   Those seeking a new life should be welcome here.

What do we want our representatives to hear?

They must resist moves by the administration to gut government control of our resources.

They must understand that if they blindly endorse Trumps actions, they will be voted out of office. They must be in favor of scrutinizing but maintaining our entitlement programs; revamping our military and support a program to reduce our National Debt. Without addressing these problems, everything else is moot. Why do we say this? Let's take a look at these individually.

Humanitarianism:

How does the candidate view immigration?

If we are to turn the tide on the current persecution of immigrants, we need to select candidates who believe in the fair and equitable treatment of every human being.

Trump has fostered racial and religious prejudice in our society and has emboldened white nationalists in the U.S. to become more vocal.

Congressman Steve King, Republican Representative from Iowa, tweeted recently, referring to Geert Wilders, the Netherlands far-right populist:

March 13th, 1:31 PM
Wilders understands that culture and demographics are our destiny. We can't restore our civilization with somebody else's babies.

The tweet drew an immediate response from Representative John Lewis:

"This is bigoted and racist. It suggests there is one tradition & one appearance that all humanity should conform to."

Congressman King is a member of the House of Representatives, but he is not representative of the beliefs of the majority of Iowans. He is exactly the type of politician that should be voted out office.

If the past few years have been about rebellion against deadlock, cronyism and polarization, it is time to recognize where our attention is desperately needed. As we try to pay for our citizen's welfare and our "Big Stick" military mentality, it is time to face facts: we cannot afford to continue building debt if we want our country to survive in its' current form. The Republicans believe the answer to this problem lies in cutting the cost of entitlement programs to balance the budget. This is totally the wrong approach. We cannot cut the cost of entitlements in any significant way without creating a hardship for millions of our citizens. The answer lies in cutting military expenses and increasing income. We cannot retreat to the past, we must move on to the future by electing candidates who are not only anti-Trump, but share a concern for fiscal responsibility and have the guts to fight for it. That means creating a positive cash flow now, not somewhere down the road. Our Debt is enormous, interest rates are rising, our defense spending is out of control, and our entitlements are overwhelming. Being a "Republican", or a "Democrat", is not enough to warrant being elected to office. We need candidates who are committed to change – changing how we fund the military – changing how we support those in need and changing how we tax ourselves to pay for it all.

What is the candidates' viewpoint on entitlements?

When we speak of "Entitlements", what do we actually mean? What are the government functions that comprise this category and how did we arrive at this point in time with the entitlement programs that currently exist? Following is a history of the development of a social conscience for America.

History: The Birth of Entitlements:

For the first one hundred and fifty years in the history of our nation, we were like a newborn child. So much to explore – the wonderment of new frontiers – development of our resources – building of our cities – "a war to end all wars" – we were a "rugged individualist" country with opportunity for anyone willing to make a commitment to their dream of independence.

As a nation, we have enjoyed the benefits of free enterprise and entrepreneurship. We owe much of the progress made over the past two hundred years to the courage and talent of individuals who tackled problems and found solutions in building the business powerhouse that is America. But success comes with responsibility, and the rugged individualists who created millions of jobs now have the responsibility to work with our elected officials to find solutions to our fiscal problems.

It was not until the great depression of the late 20's early 30's that reality set in. It was a time when even those who were willing to work and had the ability to accomplish the task were unable to find work and they and their families were suffering with nowhere to turn. Rich and poor alike were caught in this sea of nothingness. There were no jobs and there was no relief. They had few alternatives to going hungry for themselves and their families.

In the early 1930's, with the country in the midst of the worst depression in history, President Franklin D. Roosevelt initiated a series of programs to help the unemployed and destitute, many of which survive today. Known as the "New Deal" it formed the basis for a complete makeover of our society. The most notable was the Social Security Act, SSA, but there was a myriad of additional Acts which changed America forever. Among them; The Emergency Banking Act and the FDIC, The Federal Emergency Relief Administration, or FERA, The Civilian Conservation Corps, CCC, The Federal Securities Act, SEC, The National Industrial Recovery Act, precursor of the NLRB, The Works Progress Administration, WPA, The Farm Security Administration, FSA, The National Labor Relations Act and The Fair Labor Standards Act. The concept of caring for the less fortunate members of our society was foreign to most Americans at the time, but has now become the standard by which we live.

During his four terms as President, FDR transformed the country from its rugged individualist heritage to one of concern for the elderly, the sick and the unemployed. The SSA provided help for the elderly and the disabled. It was meant to be self-funding and began with a payroll deduction tax of 2% on an employee's first $3,000.00 of wages. It now taxes on the first $113,700.00 of wages at the rate of 12.4% plus a 2.9% tax for Medicare. The tax is split evenly between the employer and employee, with each paying one half the amount of the tax. The SSA is the only entitlement program which is self funded. Since its inception, the program has collected over 19 Trillion and paid out about 16 Trillion, leaving a current surplus of 2.8 Trillion at the end of 2015. Problem is, the fund is projected to be deleted by 2034 based on current demographics.

Other programs created by FDR which have survived are the FDIC which regulates banks and insures bank deposits, the SEC which oversees the stock market, the NLRB which monitors relations between labor and management and The Fair Labor Standards Act which regulates child labor laws and the minimum wage.

Following the period of rapid enactment of social programs under FDR, the next period of major program enactment occurred during an unprecedented bi-partisan cooperative period in Washington following the tragic assassination of President John F. Kennedy. When Lyndon B. Johnson assumed the presidency in 1963, he was able to push through several social programs which had been stalled in Congress during President Kennedy's tenure. The Civil Rights Act was passed in 1964 and the Voting Rights Act in 1965. The Immigration and Nationality Services Act was also passed in 1965. The Economic Opportunity Act of 1964 was Johnsons' effort in the "War on Poverty".

On July 30, 1965, President Lyndon B. Johnson signed into law amendments to the Social Security Program that created Medicare and Medicaid. Also signed into law in 1965 by President Johnson was legislation identified as the Pell Grant to help college undergraduates of low-income families.

The "Great Society" was now well underway and would forever change the way Americans lived and regarded their fellow citizens.

The Humanizing of America

Our country has progressed through the stage of "Individualism" to one of concern for our fellow man. The humanitarian concern for our citizens is admirable and necessary, but the desire to help everyone in need has created a myriad of aid programs with little concern for the long range cost of the total bundle.

The "Affordable Care Act", currently under siege and to be replaced by the "American Health Care Act" if the Republicans can cobble together a replacement, has provided health coverage for those millions of Americans who were unable to obtain it, but there is no funding program to cover the costs inherent in establishing a program of this scope. The pool of newly insured candidates is made up from a high percentage of older, less healthy candidates utilizing the Medicaid payment provision to finance their premiums, while the healthy individuals have opted to pay the penalty rather than join the program.

Social programs which comprise "entitlements" and are now active:

Social Security: If you meet the employment requirements for the program, you can begin to receive a monthly payment beginning at age 62 and continuing until your death. Your surviving spouse will then collect the payment. Currently, there are more than forty five MILLION recipients of monthly payments.

Social Security Disability Insurance: If you meet the eligibility requirements for this program, you will receive a monthly payment for your disability. Currently, there are more than ten MILLION recipients of monthly payments.

Social Security Income: If you meet the eligibility requirements for this program, you will receive a monthly payment to supplement your income. Currently, there are more than eight MILLION recipients of monthly payments.

Medicare: If you meet the eligibility requirements for this program, the majority of your medical expenses will be paid by Medicare. Currently, there are more than fifty MILLION recipients of Medicare payments.

Medicaid: If you meet the eligibility requirements for this program, your medical expenses will be paid or you may receive a subsidy on your health insurance premium. Currently, more than sixty MILLION enrolled in the program, not including those being enrolled through the Affordable Care Act.

MERHCF: Medicare Eligible Retiree Health Care Fund, established to provide funds for health benefits for military retirees and family members. Currently, it is estimated over two MILLION retirees, dependants and survivors are eligible.

Children's Health Insurance Program: CHIP, provides health insurance to children in families with incomes too high to qualify for Medicaid, but who are unable to afford private coverage. Currently, 7.6 MILLION children are enrolled in the program.

Supplemental Nutrition Assistance Program: SNAP, provides assistance in the form of food stamps and cash for low-income individuals and families. Currently, there are more than forty seven MILLION participants in the program.

Affordable Care Act: Low income individuals and families can obtain subsidies from Medicaid to enable them to receive coverage under the affordable care act. The Congressional Budget Office estimates the number of subsidized participants in the Health Insurance Exchanges will grow by 12 MILLION each year. This total is not included in the sixty Million existing participants in Medicaid.

Unemployment Compensation: Provides a weekly payment to workers who lose their job. Originally benefits were provided for 26 weeks, but have been extended for an additional 47 weeks in most cases. The Congressional Budget Office estimates 14 million workers were receiving benefits in 2009 and the total cost for the past five years: - $520 Billion.

Veteran's benefits and services: The President's 2014 Budget provides for 152.7 BILLION dollars to cover medical services and support payments to over six million veterans.

Earned Income Tax Credit: EITC, provides for a cash payment or tax credit for low income workers, especially those with children. In 2013, eligible participants numbered 27 million Americans at a cost of more than fifty six billion dollars.

Subsequent to 1965, many additional health and welfare programs have been enacted, but there was no major change in the overall landscape until the Patient Protection and Affordable Care Act, commonly called "Obamacare" was signed into law by President Obama on March 23, 2010. The cost of this program and the new *American Health Care Act* has seen a major revamping of Medicaid expenses due to the subsidy of health insurance premiums.

Entitlement Spending by Year

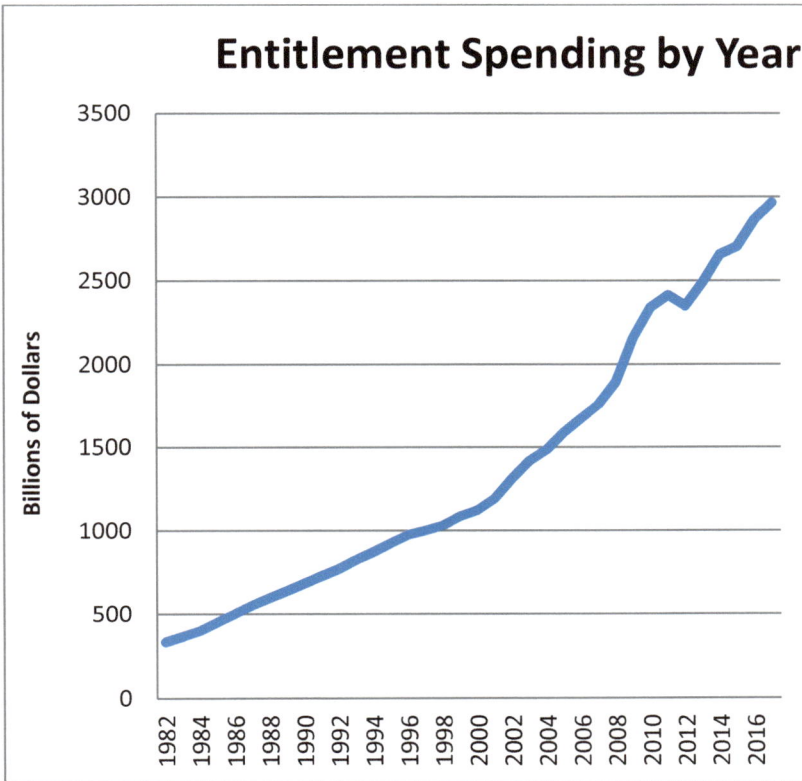

Data is from the following source: National Income and Product Accounts. Budget of the United States Fiscal Year 2017: Bureau of Economic Analysis

Please refer to the preceding chart which illustrates the growth of entitlement programs over the past thirty four years.

The total cost of programs to support the elderly, the poor, the sick, the disabled, our children, education and our veterans represents 88% of our total anticipated revenue and it does not include our military budget or the interest on the national debt, among many other items in the budget.

The six categories into which our entitlement programs are grouped and the growth in each is illustrated in the following chart. The cost and the growth of the Earned Income Tax Credit program are not included in the six categories which are shown.

Entitlement Spending by Category

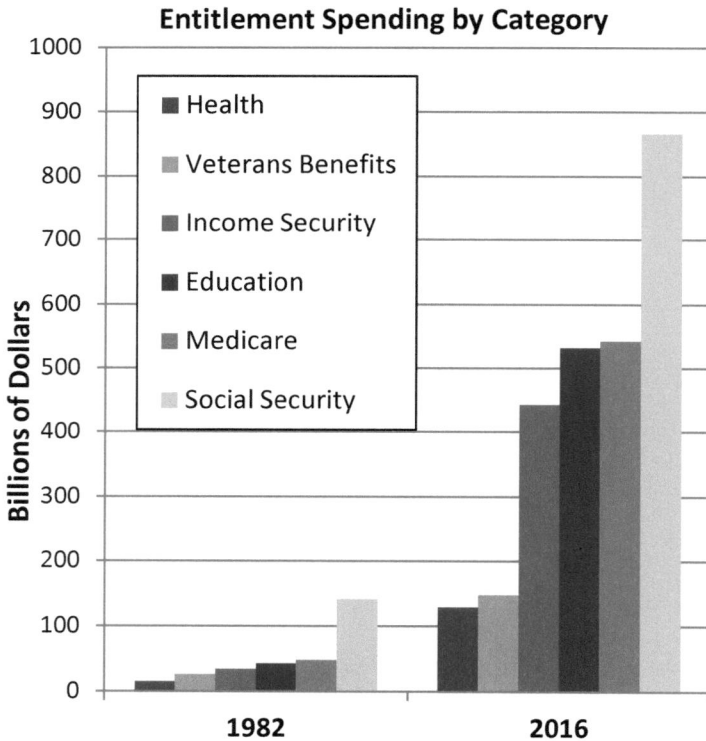

Data is from the following website:
http://www.bea.gov/national/nipaweb/Ni_FedBeaSna/TableView.asp?SelectedTable=7

The six categories of entitlement are comprised of the following:

Social Security: The original social assistance program to help older citizens, disabled workers and survivors of beneficiaries who have been employed and have contributed into the program. It is the only social program other than Medicare which was designed to be self-funding with contributions from workers and their employers. Currently, the social security trust fund has almost three Trillion dollars. The fund is entirely invested in U.S. Government Securities at an interest rate of 3.628 percent.

Medicare: The other "self-funded" program provides health insurance for seniors 65 years and older and for persons with disabilities. The Medicare trust fund currently totals 287 Billion dollars. An adjunct to Medicare is the Medicaid Program administered by the Centers for Medicare and Medicaid Services, (CMS). Medicaid was created in 1965 to help provide low-income families with health insurance. Persons who are blind, disabled, pregnant or aged are eligible for coverage. ObamaCare has greatly expanded the role of Medicaid for low-income workers through the Health Exchanges.

Education, Training, Employment and Social Services:
Program services include funding for the National Endowment for the Arts, the National endowment for the Humanities, the Smithsonian Institution, the John F. Kennedy Center for the Performing Arts, the National Gallery of Art, the Corporation for Public Broadcasting and the Library of Congress. It also provides funding for the Department of Education, training programs for the Department of Labor, and social service programs for the Department of Health and Human Services.

Income Security: Provides cash or similar help to low-income citizens for assistance with housing, energy or nutrition. Unemployment insurance, food stamps, foster care and Supplemental Security Income. Federal retirement and disability programs are also funded in this category.

Veterans Benefits and Services: Primarily covers veterans' medical care, pensions, education and rehabilitation benefits and housing assistance through the Department of Veteran Affairs, the VA. The Department of Labor's Veterans' Employment and Training Service is also funded by this function.

Health: This function includes the National Institute of Health, (NIH), The Food and Drug Administration, Centers for Disease Control and Prevention, Medicaid, the State Children's Health Insurance Program, (SCHIP), and health care for federal workers and retirees'.

The rapid and rampant expansion of these programs has placed us in a precarious position considering our current debt and income. Robert D. Reischauer, Director of the Congressional Budget Office, testified before the Bipartisan Committee on Entitlement and Tax Reform on July 15, 1994 – Over twenty years ago – The message he tried to get across to the Congress was that entitlement spending could not be sustained at the then current levels without driving the budget to unsustainable deficits. Unfortunately, Congress chose to ignore the warnings and now, twenty three years later, we will have to bite the bullet.   Following are excerpts from his testimony:

> *"Spending on entitlement programs is the major factor underlying the overall deterioration of the deficit situation projected during the next several decades."*

"Large budget deficits are debilitating because they absorb national saving that otherwise could be used for investments that would improve the living standards of future generations."

"The hemorrhaging in the deficit that will occur after about 2010 under current policies is also clearly related to the anticipated increase in spending on entitlements."

"We could reap enormous benefits in the future by taking only modest, prudent steps to modify current spending and taxing policies. Such changes made now would produce increasing gains in deficit reduction and national saving in the decades ahead. Moreover, the adverse impacts could be spread over a larger number of cohorts, and because the changes could be phased in over a number of years, they need not cause major disruptions in life styles or standards of living."

"If we fail to act soon, however, this opportunity will pass and the required actions will have to be more drastic. Previously available options for reducing benefits will become less viable, for example, because members of the baby-boom generation will no longer have time to adjust their work and saving behavior in response to cuts in their benefits. Yet the budgetary shortfalls will mount, and the need to respond will grow commensurately. As difficult as the policy choices are now, they will only get worse the longer this action is postponed."[1]

The "hemorrhaging" in the deficit that Mr. Reischauer predicted if entitlements were not cut back was based on a prediction by the CBO that total entitlements would increase by a total of 736

---

[1] Robert D. Reischauer, Director of the Congressional Budget Office, testified before the Bipartisan Committee on Entitlement and Tax Reform on July 15, 1994

BILLION over the ten year period from 1994 to 2004. Their worst fears were realized and entitlements reached one trillion, 486 Billion for 2004. This year the total is expected to increase by one Trillion, 855 Billion from the 1994 total. These amounts are completely unsustainable and the "modest, prudent steps" envisioned by the CBO in 1994 to contain the growth in entitlements must now become much "more drastic", to use the CBO's phraseology.

It remains to be seen how the American Health Care Act will resolve this problem. Trump's promise: If you have Health Care under the ACA, you will have coverage under the AHCA.

The Affordable Care Act (ACA) has led to 20 million Americans gaining health coverage, many for the first time ever. In the first quarter of 2016, the uninsured rate reached a record low of 8.6 percent of Americans. These gains are expected to grow as individuals continue to enroll in coverage through the Health Insurance Marketplaces ("Marketplaces") and more states participate in Medicaid expansion.

This data raises a few questions:

1. Can our Medical Support Infrastructure handle the increased load which is being placed upon it by the newly insured individuals?
2. What will be the unintended consequences of adding 24 million people to the health care rolls each year?
3. What will be the unintended consequences of adding 12-13 million people to Medicaid/CHIP each year?

As a society, do we want our elderly to have sufficient funds for food, clothing and shelter? Do we want our unemployed to be able to sustain a decent lifestyle until they are able to find work? Do we want our sick children to be cared for? Do we want the poor and the elderly to have access to medical care? Do we want to provide assistance to needy families in times of distress? Do we want to help bright young students obtain higher education?

The majority of Americans would answer "yes" to each of these questions. The problem then becomes one of funding. With the massive debt we are facing, in addition to the yearly deficits we are incurring, how can we do all these things? The answer is simple. We must drastically reduce our military budget and survey each of our entitlement programs to insure the money is being spent on the purpose intended when the programs were initiated. We must then create a budget that enables us to pay the interest on our debt as well as funding the entitlement programs and still begin to pay down the national debt.

There is little we can do immediately to reduce the cost of entitlements. Each and every program must be evaluated, investigated and scrutinized to determine where waste can be eliminated and efficiencies can be obtained. We must work diligently to bring every program into compliance with its stated purpose. This can only be accomplished with the support of the electorate. Substantial change will not be possible until the American people become aware of the situation. When they realize the true nature of the situation, they will demand action. It cannot occur from the top down.   It must be from the bottom up.

How did we get into this situation?

Too much military, too much welfare and too little income. We must reduce our military budget, but that will not be enough to solve the problem. We need to cut welfare programs **or** increase income. Since cutting welfare programs is neither desirable nor possible, we must increase income. We will look at solutions to that problem later.

Revamping the Military:

President Trump wants to increase our military budget by 54 Billion Dollars! This is insane. The budget should be reduced to little more than half its current level, not increased. We need to address our "Military mentality".

We spend more on our military than the combined total spent by the rest of the civilized world. *We could cut our budget in half* and it would still exceed the combined total spent by Russia and China! Does this make sense to spend the amount of money on our military that we currently spend? Of course not!

Our military budget must reflect a "defense" orientation rather than a "remake the world in our image" strategy.

Does our candidate share our view on The Military?

History:

Our country was founded by individualists who believed they should be free to work and enjoy the fruit of their labors, and that freedom should be protected with their life, if necessary.

Early on, the threats to our freedom were easy to identify. Imperial nations that believed they had a right to our property. Great Britain, France and Spain attempted to overthrow our government. We repulsed each of these attacks with the resolve of a newly free people protecting their property.

When Europe erupted into war in August, 1914, the entire European Continent eventually became embroiled in the conflict. German U-boats sank seven U.S merchant ships and the British ocean liner RMS Lusitania. With financial interests in Great Britain and France, the United States declared war on Germany on April 6, 1917.

The entry of the U.S. into WWI was the first time the full military resources of the country had been committed to war on foreign soil. The rational – fight them in Europe, or fight them on American soil. That theory seemed reasonable at the time.

Following WWI, the country grew at an accelerating pace. The Midwest became the manufacturing center of the world. New York was establishing itself as the financial capital of the world. Our economic might could not be matched by any other country.

On Sunday, December 7, 1941, Japan attacked Pearl Harbor, dealing a catastrophic blow to our Pacific Fleet, killing 2402 Americans. The next day, President Franklin Delano Roosevelt addressed Congress and called December 7, 1941 "**A Date Which Will Live In Infamy**". A declaration of war with Japan was approved by Congress that day. Two days later, Congress declared war with Germany and Italy. Pearl Harbor was a test of America's resolve. Our manufacturing plants were immediately converted to producing the goods of war. Tanks, Aircraft and Guns poured off the assembly lines. The country mobilized every conceivable asset for the war effort. The result was astounding. America's unity and resolve had propelled it into a juggernaut of fighting might. On May 8, 1945, Germany surrendered and on September 1st, 1945, Japan surrendered, thus ended the greatest worldwide conflict of modern history. Americans were proud of our country. We took a catastrophic blow to our naval force and came back to vanquish the aggressor in less than four years. An astounding accomplishment!

The mobilization of our resources following the Japanese attack produced the most dynamic and powerful war machine ever created in the history of the world. In a few short years our country was converted from a sleeping giant into a military power of unequaled capacity. We were united by a single purpose – defeat the aggressor who had attacked us in such a cowardly manner while portraying a desire for peace.

In the aftermath of war, converting factories back to producing civilian goods was accomplished with almost as much speed as the war conversions. After five years of putting the nation's defense ahead of their own needs, consumers eagerly snatched up products as they became available. The military, having grown to the greatest fighting force ever known, did not easily return to reasonable size. Our military prowess remained at an unusually high level and we found ourselves becoming involved in one skirmish after another.

Somewhere along the way, our creed to defend our country came to mean defend all countries, near of far, democratic or dictatorial. As the world's enforcer of democracy, the lifeblood of our nation has been weakened by a series of ill conceived and ill fated encounters. Korea, Viet Nam, Afghanistan and Iraq along with many smaller "interventions" have taken a toll in lives and resources. The presumed purpose of these costly wars was to stop the spread of Communism or terrorist organizations, but the cost of these incursions has been horrific in lives lost and assets wasted. Because we were capable of squandering these resources does not make a case for intervention.

Should we be the World's Police Force?

Military Expenditures by Nations of the World

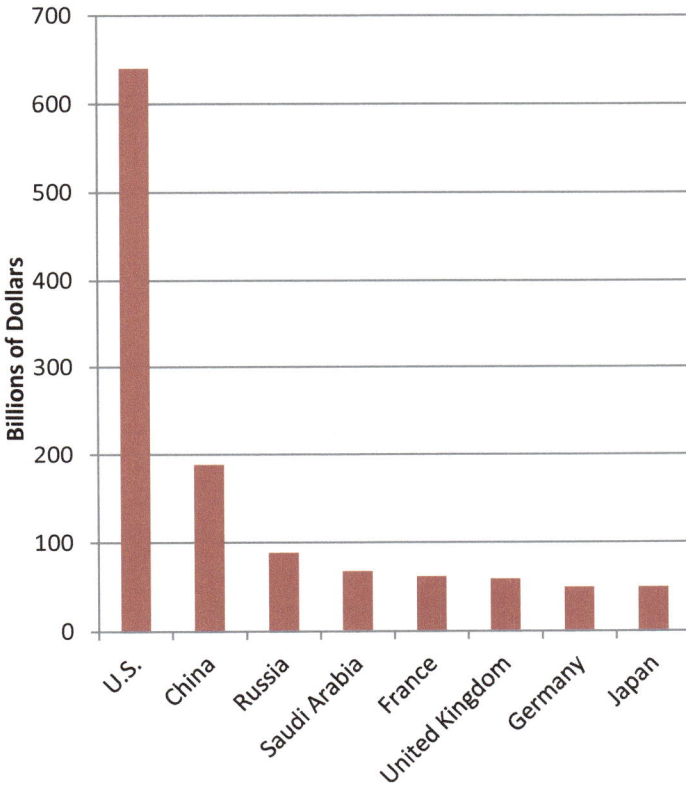

The chart above illustrates the disproportional spending by the U.S. when compared to the other nations of the world.

When North Korea invaded South Korea on June 25, 1950, we sent 300,000 troops to Korea to "stop the spread of Communism". Over 36,000 U.S. military were killed before an armistice was signed on July 27, 1953.

---

[2] Stockholm International Peace Research Institute

The concept of committing American troops to combat wherever in the world there was a threat to democratic rule had now been established. The cost of this policy in the lives lost and broken as well as the financial burden on the country is almost immeasurable. *We cannot and we should not be the world's police force.* Following World War II we gravitated toward the position of being the world's keeper. Isolationism had been knocked out of the national psych.

Adapt or die also applies to nations. If any doubts remain concerning the wisdom of sending American soldiers into combat in conditions which are totally foreign them, the recent experience in Iraq and Afghanistan should dispel any lingering questions.

If an argument really had to be made against foreign intervention by American troops, consider what the tremendous investment in lives and dollars has produced in the Middle East with Iraq, Afghanistan, Syria, etc.   Little permanent improvement can be claimed as a result of these heartbreaking sacrifices.

The futility of sending fighting forces into distant foreign countries is illustrated by a brief review of U.S, involvement in foreign wars:

1950-1953 – Korean War: The United States responded to North Korean invasion of South Korea by going to its assistance, pursuant to United Nations Security Council resolutions. US forces deployed in Korea exceeded 300,000 during the last year of the conflict. Over 36,600 US military were killed in action. Total Cost 1950-1953: 320 Billion

1955–64 – Vietnam: First military advisors sent to Vietnam in 1955. By 1964, US troop levels had grown to 21,000. On 7 August 1964, US Congress approved Gulf of Tonkin resolution affirming "All necessary measures to repel any armed attack against the forces of the United States and to prevent further aggression and assist any member or protocol state of the SEATO defense treaty requesting assistance.

1959–75 – Vietnam War: US military advisers had been in South Vietnam for a decade, and their numbers had been increased as the military position of the Saigon government became weaker. After citing what he termed were attacks on US destroyers in the Tonkin Gulf, President Johnson asked in August 1964 for a resolution expressing US determination to support freedom and protect peace in Southeast Asia. Congress responded with the Tonkin Gulf Resolution, expressing support for "all necessary measures" the President might take to repel armed attacks against US forces and prevent further aggression. Following this resolution, and following a communist attack on a US installation in central Vietnam, the United States escalated its participation in the war to a peak of 543,000 military personnel by April 1969. Total Cost 1965-1975: 686 Billion

1990-1991 – Persian Gulf War: Primarily an Air-War ordered by President George H.W. Bush, a massive offensive effort drove the Iraqi forces out of Kuwait in little over six months of fighting. The conflict was known as "Operation Desert Storm", and involved a total of 700,000 Allied troops of which over 500,000 were from the U.S. Total Cost 1990-1991: 96 Billion.

2003–2011 – War in Iraq: March 20, 2003. The United States leads a coalition that includes Britain, Australia and Spain to invade Iraq with the stated goal being to disarm Iraq in pursuit of peace, stability, and security both in the Gulf region and in the United States. (Operation Iraqi Freedom).

2010-11 - War in Iraq: On February 17, 2010, U.S. Secretary of Defense Robert Gates announced that as of September 1, 2010, the name "Operation Iraqi Freedom" would be replaced by "Operation New Dawn". This coincides with the reduction of American troops to 50,000.

2001 – Afghanistan War: Operation Enduring Freedom began in October, 2001, US Armed Forces invade Afghanistan in response to 9/11 terrorist attacks and begin combat action in Afghanistan against Al Qaeda terrorists and their Taliban supporters.

Total Cost of the war in Afghanistan is combined with the cost of the Iraq war as the Federal Budget combines these costs in many instances. According to "The Cost of Wars" Project, an initiative based at Brown University's Watson Institute for International Studies, the cost of the Iraq and Afghanistan Wars has resulted in 6,656 U.S. troops killed and 106,000 wounded. The total cost of the two wars is 3.1 Trillion dollars with an additional 884.4 Billion dollars in obligations to be paid in the future. These are horrendous numbers of human suffering and economic sacrifice.

The total number of active military personnel, including Army, Navy, Marine Corps and Air Force is now 1,422,600. Add to that total the Army, Navy, Marine Corps, Air Force Reserves and the Army and Air National Guard of 1,100,000 and you have a military force numbering over 2,500,000.

During the twelve years of combat in the Iraq and Afghanistan wars, over two million military personnel were deployed in the two conflicts. The number of returning combatants requiring and seeking disability aid has reached unprecedented levels. Recent figures from the Veterans Administration indicate that as many as 750,000 have applied for or are receiving disability benefits. The ratio of Iraq and Afghanistan veterans seeking physical or mental compensation is more than four times the average rate of veterans seeking disability in all of our previous wars dating back almost one hundred years ago to World War I, (The war to end all wars).

There have been many theories advanced to explain the flood of claims for war related injuries and trauma suffered in "Operation Enduring Freedom" and "Operation Iraqi Freedom". Researchers have studied the effects of post traumatic stress disorder, (PTSD), delayed-onset PTSD, malingering and economics, but there has not been any definitive explanation to account for the huge surge in claims for disability among Iraq and Afghanistan veterans.

The answer to this riddle should not be so elusive. Consider the consequences of sending American forces into a country where the culture is foreign, the terrain is foreign, the language is foreign and the enemy is a shadow. All of their previous experiences which trigger danger alerts are useless in an environment which is totally foreign and death can come from anywhere at any time. Is it really any wonder that exposure to these conditions produces stress?

We simply cannot continue to play the type of war games which have produced these results.

We should not allocate resources to a military establishment that is stuck in the 19th century. The concepts upon which we are basing our military objectives must be reexamined. We cannot continue to interject ourselves into every perceived threat to the autonomy of nations throughout the world.

Our national political culture must be redefined to aid those in need with humanitarian assistance and stop trying to subvert political regimes which are not in our likeness. A case in point: The fiasco by the U.S. Agency for International Development. The Associated Press uncovered the plot by the U.S. government to undermine the Cuban Communist Government. Through a network of independent contractors, USAID funded the set up of a "Cuban Twitter" network called ZunZuneo to dupe users into thinking they were signing up to a social networking site. According to the AP, over 1.5 million was spent on the project to give the illusion of a legitimate business, including the creation of a website so subscribers could send their text messages to groups of their choice.

Once the network had built up a Cuban audience of mostly young people, the plan was to promote them into dissent against the Cuban government.

Really? Is this what our country stands for? Have we become immune to our governments' meddling in the internal affairs of other countries? This story would be completely unbelievable were it not for the Iran Contra Affair, when the U.S. secretly sold arms to Iran in spite of an arms embargo and used the money to fund the anti-communist rebels in Nicaragua. Unfortunately, these stories are only the ones which make their way onto the news networks. The U.S. has been involved in covert operations for many years, mostly as directed by the CIA. The CIA has been actively involved in attempts to overthrow the governments which were perceived to be "not like ours" is a long list. In just the past 15 years it includes Iraq, Afghanistan, Venezuela, Haiti, Gaza, Somalia, Iran, Libra, Syria and Ukraine. Doesn't this amount to treason? The definition of treason is "the offense of acting to overthrow one's government". We can't impose "freedom" on other societies. Tyrannical and dictatorial governments eventually are brought down without help from "foreigners". The United States Agency for International Development states that its aim is to "work to end extreme global poverty and enable resilient, democratic societies to realize their potential." It appears that is a euphemism for "we will enable you to overthrow your government".

Aid, given freely, is admirable. Aid, given with subversion as its goal, is reprehensible. We need to retool our foreign policy toward compassion and forget about trying to overthrow governments not to our liking.

Our government has run roughshod over the rights of the citizens of the world for much too long. We have to think about how our American ideals have been warped and usurped by a small number of elitists in the government. America is scorned by many of the worlds' inhabitants because of our meddling in the affairs of their nation while ostensibly offering help.

It just doesn't make economic sense for one country to invade the territorial rights of another country. History tells us that the cost/benefit ratio of warfare has seldom been worth the investment for the aggressor.

Our energies should be marshaled entirely toward developing armed forces which are truly "defensive" forces in every sense of the word. We can do this at a fraction of the current military budget. We do not need resources to send to Iraq, or Afghanistan, or Syria, or anywhere else *except* as a part of a U.N. effort. We need only defensive forces sufficient to convince any potential aggressor that the "gain would not be worth the pain".

If this country is to survive, and provide the social services our citizens deserve, we must stop spending for military attack forces and ease the tax burden on our businesses and individuals to provide the funds necessary for them to compete in the world economy. It is not in the best interests of this nation to continue to play the role of "world enforcer".

We can regain our position of pre-eminence in world affairs if we follow a policy of humanitarianism: Helping those countries that need and want our help.

We live in an inter-connected world community. Our commitment to world peace and the fair treatment of all members of the world's society must be as part of the United Nation's Peace Keeping Force.

Trump's missile response to Assad was totally wrong. As horrific as Assad's crime, we cannot be judge, jury and executioner. We are not the World's Police Force. This is "Big Stick" Military force wielded without the authority of the world community. . This path has resulted in creating a military elite in our country. Assad's heinous actions cannot be ignored, but we must convince our partners in the UN that military action should be taken before we commit our forces to the response. Our participation should be in proportion to that of the other members.

We cannot and should not "go it alone".

Our Defense Department's concept of how our military force should be configured, and how it should be deployed is based on "old school" theory.

Unfortunately, President Trump views the military as an extension of his ego with aircraft carriers, ships, planes and every piece of hardware one uses to play war games. A reduction of any amount in the military budget while he is our President is going to be difficult. Hopefully, Congress will rein in his fantasies before irreparable harm can occur, and meaningful changes to our military can be made following his departure.

In his pamphlet published January 10, 1776, Thomas Paine wrote "Being a part of Britain would drag America into unnecessary European wars and keep it from the international commerce at which America excelled. The pamphlet was titled "Common Sense".

What are the principles of defense upon which our country was founded? Let's look at the Constitution:

THE CONSTITUTION OF THE UNITED STATES:
Preamble:
We the People of the United States, in Order to form a more perfect Union, establish Justice, insure domestic Tranquility, provide for the common defence, promote the general Welfare, and secure the Blessings of Liberty to ourselves and our Posterity, do ordain and establish this Constitution for the United States of America.

"PROVIDE FOR THE COMMON DEFENCE" – what does this mean?

Do you think they had Iraq or Afghanistan in mind? Or Libya, or Syria, or Ukraine? I don't think so. Their concept of defence did not encompass sending troops to fight other peoples' battles.

How far can we stretch the belief in common defence? Should it mean attempting to convert all of the countries of the world to our concept of liberty? Should it mean attempting to convert any country in the world to our concept of liberty? If we judge a nation's people are subjected to tyranny, it is not our obligation to free them from such a predicament without the sanction of the U.N.

How Do We Do It?

We cannot and we should not be the worlds' police force. We have a responsibility to ourselves to maintain a strong and viable nation and we can't do that by building armed forces capable of fighting wars in all corners of the world.

We should be able to accomplish this with a military budget which would be a fraction of the current amount. For 2017, the base budget for the military is 523.9 BILLION plus 58.8 BILLION for "overseas contingency operations". Trump wants another 54

Billion! According to the Department of Defense, this budget would allow them to "sustain U.S. global leadership and shape the Joint Force to be prepared to confront and defeat aggression anywhere in the world". This then is the problem. It is "anywhere in the world" that defines the philosophy of our military. We have to get out of the "policing the world" business and concentrate on the defense of our country.

A "Defense only" force could reduce our current military budget by slightly more than half. We would save 300 Billion dollars a year, leaving a budget of 273 Billion – an amount still greater than the military budgets of China and Russia combined!

The DoD maintains an overall military end strength of 2,238,400, personnel that the DoD considers "Warfighters". In addition, family support needs of its "Warfighters", requires another 8.5 BILLION for child care, morale, welfare and recreation and spousal employment.

Maintaining a fighting force of over two million members is totally "out of whack" with the concept of a military based on the principle of defense.

We need new thinking in how Congress views our military establishment. We cannot become embroiled in other countries conflicts except as part of a United Nations multi-national force. We should always do what we can to alleviate suffering wherever it occurs, but militarily we should mind our own business. Aggression, regardless of who the perpetrator is, is economically unfeasible in today's world. Our national security policy should fulfill one purpose and one purpose only – to make it absolutely unthinkable for anyone to attack our sovereignty. What do we need to accomplish this?

Suggestions for a revamped military:

1. A well trained military force for the exclusive purpose of defending our country and a task force designed to join in U.N. military operations when required.

2. Nuclear submarines with strike capabilities to hit any target on earth.

3. Improved anti-missile defense system.

4. A first class intelligence system with ears in all corners of the world. We must know of plans before they become actions.

5. A small, nimble strike force to protect our interests anywhere on the globe, capable of entering a foreign country where our citizens are in danger and neutralizing the threat.

6. A naval force of fast, maneuverable ships designed to deliver a strike force. Get in – Get it done – Get out.

7. Technologically advanced weaponry to counteract any threat to our homeland. This would include satellite based laser systems to pinpoint strikes on any target worldwide.

8. A Department of Cyber Security for the purpose of continuously monitoring our networks to insure their integrity.

If a country cannot be relied upon to provide safe haven for our ambassadors, we should not send them there. Countries that are deemed to be unsafe for travel by Americans should be designated as such, and American citizens should be aware that travel there would be at their risk and should not expect the government to provide protection for them.

We have a finite capacity to engage in military conflicts.

Money saved from redesigning our military can be used to help bring our budget into balance and expand our program of fighting hunger in poor nations.

The benefits would immediately begin to reflect themselves in a lower cost of doing business for the nations' businesses. Lower costs mean American products are more competitive in the world market, improving exports and job creation in this country.

What about nuclear war? Nuclear war is always a possibility, but there would be no winners, only losers. If a nuclear war were to occur, it would probably be by a mistake made by someone in control of an arsenal in this country or one of the other ICBM capable countries of the world. With the U.S., Russia, China, India, Israel and now North Korea all possessing the capability to launch a Nuclear ICBM, there is certainly the possibility of a catastrophic error occurring. To intentionally start a conflict of this nature is unlikely, as most of their country, as well as the world would likely be destroyed. The U.S. alone has more than four hundred ICBM's in silos, enough to destroy the world several times over. The likelihood of an intentional launch is highly unlikely. Of course, the assumption here is that a rational person is in control of the Nuclear Codes.

The cost/benefit ratio of war is strikingly evident when Nuclear War is considered. To attack a nation with nuclear weapons would render it useless to anyone, victor or vanquished alike.
Cost =High, Benefit = Zero.

We should concentrate our efforts on solving the problems at hand. If we are unable to muster up the courage to solve our financial problems, our country will eventually be financially owned by outsiders and we will all be working for foreign powers without a shot being fired.

The National Debt:
$19,935,316,185,835.78

It's just a number, right? It's a big number, but it's just a number, right? Wrong. It's a debt. It's money we owe and it must be paid back. Problem is, we have to pay interest on the debt. Were it not for this detail, we could ignore the whole thing. Unfortunately, we do have to pay interest, lots of it. Last year the interest cost amounted to $432,649,652,901.12, or 14 1/2 percent of our total income for the year. If our debt were to be divided equally between every working American, the amount owed per person would be $116,438.36.

But take heart! President Trump reduced the debt by 12 Billion dollars in his first month in office! If you find this hard to believe, you can read his tweet here:

February 25th, 8:19 AM
Trump Tweet: The media has not reported that the National Debt in my first month went down by $12 billion vs a $200 billion increase in Obama first mo. * *source: Fox and Friends newscast*

This would be encouraging were it not so pathetic. The National Debt fluctuates constantly due to the timing of debit and credit posting. A change of 12 billion, or .06 of 1% is merely a reflection of this process. Unfortunately, Trump's policies do not hold any hope for reducing the debt. In fact they will only accelerate the accumulation of more debt.

What is our candidates' view on the National Debt? Electing members to Congress who share our view of the importance of eliminating our National Debt is crucial.

A well known human trait is "fight or flight" in the face of imminent danger, but unfortunately we humans do not seem to possess a mechanism for threats which are not immediate, but long term. This is the situation we face with our National Debt. When we finally recognize the Debt as an imminent danger, our choices will be few and extremely painful.

We have had a budget deficit for 45 of the past 50 years. We haven't had a surplus for 14 years and our deficit for the past 8 years has averaged a staggering amount of over one Trillion dollars a year. How do we expect to stay solvent when we are generating yearly borrowing of this magnitude?

The following chart should concern you. It shows the escalating amount of money the United States owes to foreign and domestic sources. The chart covers the past 30 years. You will want to notice the rate of increase over the past ten years and especially over the past five years.

National Debt

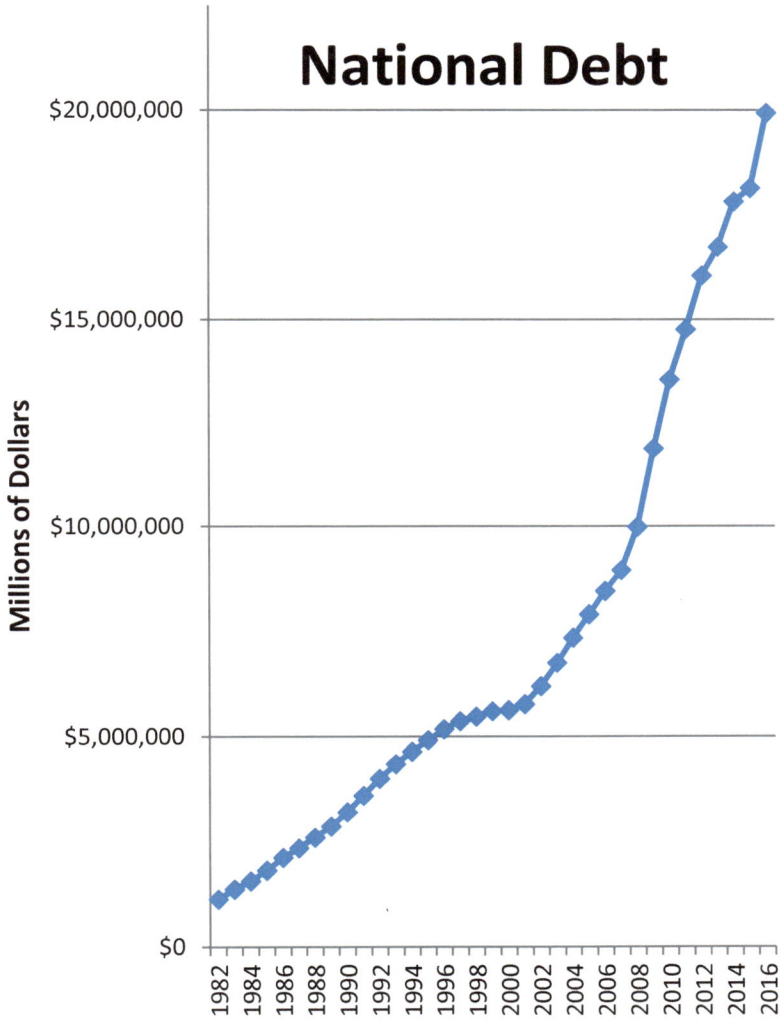

Chart showing National Debt in Millions of Dollars from 1982 to 2016, rising from approximately $1,000,000 in 1982 to nearly $20,000,000 in 2016.

[1] OMB, The White House

Over the past ten years our payments of interest on our debt have averaged more than $400 Billion dollars per year. The Fed has suppressed the interest rate for the past seven years at an unsustainable level, which has kept our interest payments somewhat manageable. The current rate the Fed is paying on the national debt averages less than two and one half percent. The Federal Funds rate is currently .66 percent. While this helps in keeping interest costs down, it does nothing to encourage banks to lend money, as can be seen from the huge accumulation of bank reserves.

To expect to maintain this low interest rate is unrealistic. The rapid growth in the nation's money supply is certain to exert pressure on interest rates. What is the money supply?

Money supply is defined by the Federal Reserve as follows:

> "The money supply is commonly defined to be a group of safe assets that households and businesses can use to make payments or to hold as short-term investments. For example, U.S. currency and balances held in checking accounts and savings accounts are included in many measures of the money supply.
>
> There are several standard measures of the money supply, including the monetary base, M1, and M2. The monetary base is defined as the sum of currency in circulation and reserve balances (deposits held by banks and other depository institutions in their accounts at the Federal Reserve). M1 is defined as the sum of currency held by the public and transaction deposits at depository institutions (which are financial institutions that obtain their funds mainly through deposits from the public, such as commercial banks, savings and loan associations, savings

banks, and credit unions). M2 is defined as M1 plus savings deposits, small-denomination time deposits (those issued in amounts of less than $100,000), and retail money market mutual fund shares." [3]

If the economy could grow as fast as the money supply, it would not present a big problem as the economy would be able to absorb the increased flow of money and still maintain equilibrium. Unfortunately, that is not the case and the Fed's policy of continually increasing the money supply at a rate in excess of the nation's economic growth will inevitably result in increasing the rate of inflation. When this occurs, the cost of money will increase and interest rates will begin to climb. This will result in higher cost of payments on the national debt and will exacerbate what is already a budgetary disaster.

Quoting from the November/December Review by the Federal Reserve Bank of St. Louis:

> *"Every major acceleration in M2 growth has been associated with a major acceleration in inflation. Likewise, every major deceleration in M2 growth has been associated with a major deceleration in inflation. Accordingly, policy makers might be making a serious mistake if the noisy short-term movements in M2 and inflation persuaded them that money does not matter anymore."* [4]

We cannot "print" our way out of this – even the U.S. government has a finite capacity for debt and we truly do not want to find out what that limit is. Each year we delay the inevitable by raising the debt limit.

---

[3] Board of Governors of The Federal Reserve System
[4] November/December Review by The Federal Reserve Bank of St. Louis

As interest rates increase, the cost of servicing our debt will require more borrowing. Our trading partners become nervous and refuse to buy our bonds, leading to higher interest bonds to entice buyers. As interest rates rise, fear of our fiscal policies grows. As these fears intensify, more nations will seek alternatives to the U.S. dollar as their reserve currency and the U.S. will lose its ability to print money with impunity, thereby exacerbating the bond cost - interest rate-money printing cycle.

In private business, when expenses exceed income, there is a shortfall which must be covered by savings, if there are any, or by borrowing, if available. Credit is extended, but at a cost. Interest charges accrue. As the amount of credit increases, interest rates increase as well. If your income is unable to cover your expenses, including interest, you need to continue to increase your borrowing as long as there are lenders willing to extend credit. Your expenses, which exceeded your income before borrowing, now become greater by the interest cost. You eventually reach a point where credit is no longer available at any price. As a nation, we could declare bankruptcy, but a more likely scenario would be printing whatever amount of money was needed to pay our commitments. This would lead to hyper- inflation and would only postpone eventual disaster.

The path the Federal Reserve has been following has left us vulnerable to an attack on the U.S. Dollar. Evidence of this can be seen by agreements between major economic players of the world to use their own currencies for inter-country trading. China, Russia, India, Turkey, Brazil and Venezuela are among the countries which have joined together to reduce their need for a U.S. reserve currency.

The global community is keeping a close eye on the economic health of our country. We cannot afford to let our financial condition deteriorate any further.

The following chart illustrates the accelerating growth in M2, Money Stock.

M2 Money Stock

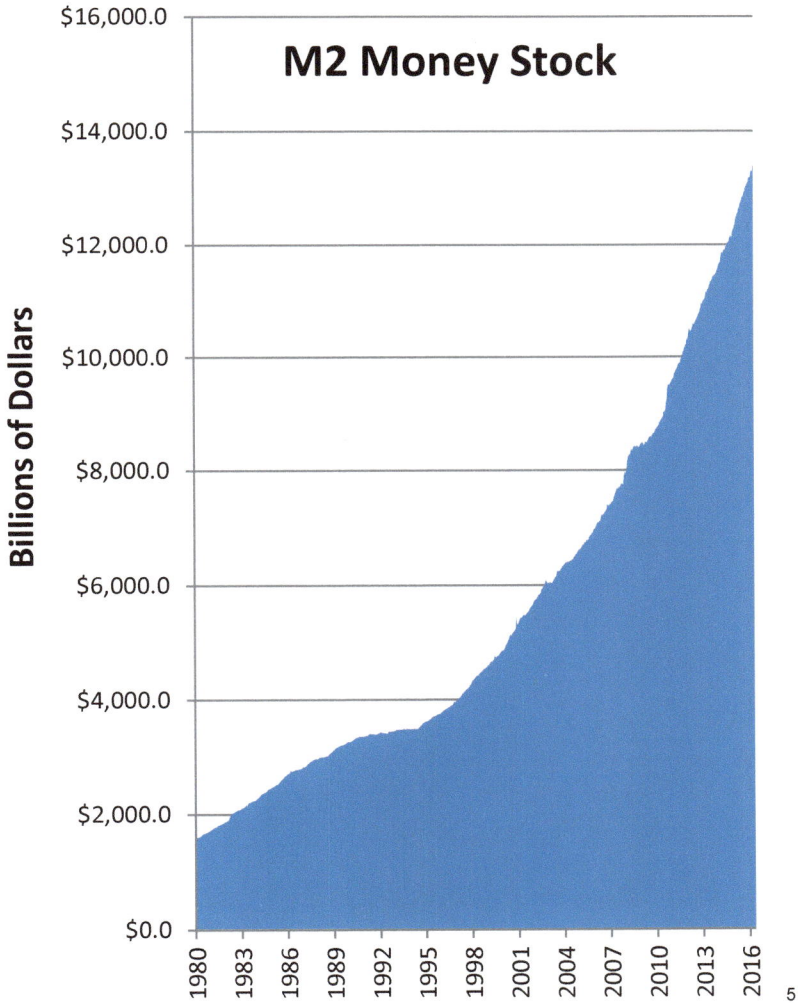

[5] Data for this chart was obtained from
https://research.stlouisfed.org/fred2/series/M2/

As great as the increase has been in the money supply, M2, it does not include the amount of excess reserves pouring into the nation's banking institutions. This is where a significant amount of the "Quantitative Easing" money has been "squirreled away".

The Federal Reserve has a financial requirement for each of the banks in its system. This is known as the "Reserve Balance Required" and it's the amount of money the bank must maintain in cash in their vault or on deposit with the Federal Reserve. At the present time, the total amount of *required reserves* held by banks is 87 BILLION dollars. This is the amount deemed necessary to conduct their business and provide sufficient cushion for times of stress.

On the other hand, the cash and deposits that the banks are holding that is not required for their normal operations, is known as "Excess Reserves". The total amount of these "Excess Reserves" now held by the banking industry is TWO TRILLION DOLLARS. This is 1.5 TRILLION dollars more in cash reserves than the banks had 8 years ago.

Since the Federal Reserve is paying interest to the banks on their excess reserves, the incentive for the banks to lend that money is little or none. Please see the following chart which shows the incredible expansion of excess reserves.

Source: Federal Reserve Bank of St. Louis
https://research.stlouisfed.org/fred2

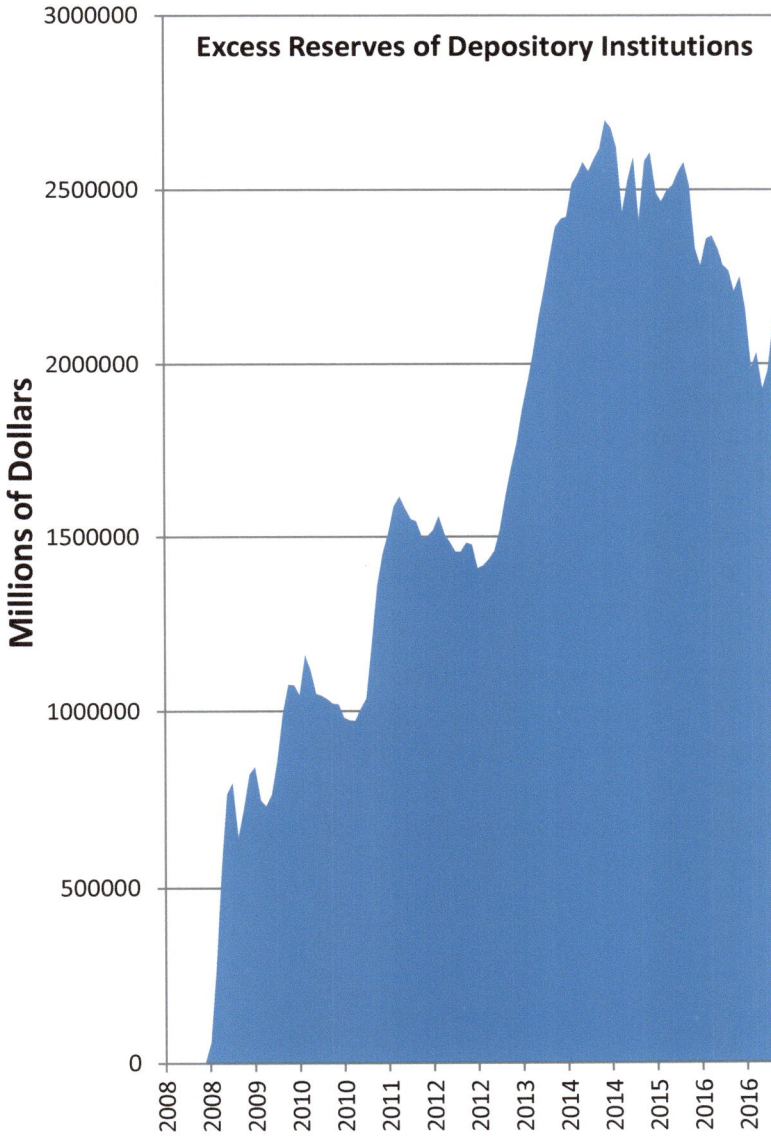

Excess Reserves of Depository Institutions

The buildup of these excess reserves by the nation's banks is creating pressure which will ultimately be relieved by the flow of money into the system, further fueling inflationary forces.

An increase in money supply which exceeds the growth rate of the economy is inflationary. Based on statistics provided by the U.S. Government, the increase in Gross Domestic Product for the U.S. economy since 2008, when the Fed began their policy of "Quantitative Easing", was 2.370 Billion dollars, or 14.1% in 8 years, or 1.76% average per year. During that same six year period the money supply, M2, increased by 4.995 Billion dollars, or 37.9%, an average of 4.7%per year. In other words, the money supply increased TWICE as fast as the ability of the economy to absorb it.

The following chart illustrates the actual economic growth as indicated by our Gross Domestic Product, GDP, in chained 2009 dollars for the past nine years.

While GDP growth has been minimal, as is evident from this chart, growth in Money Supply, M2, as previously noted has been expanding at a much faster rate. While GDP growth has shown improvement recently, there is little likelihood of it expanding sufficiently over the next few years to enable us to avoid inflationary pressures.

Gross Domestic Product

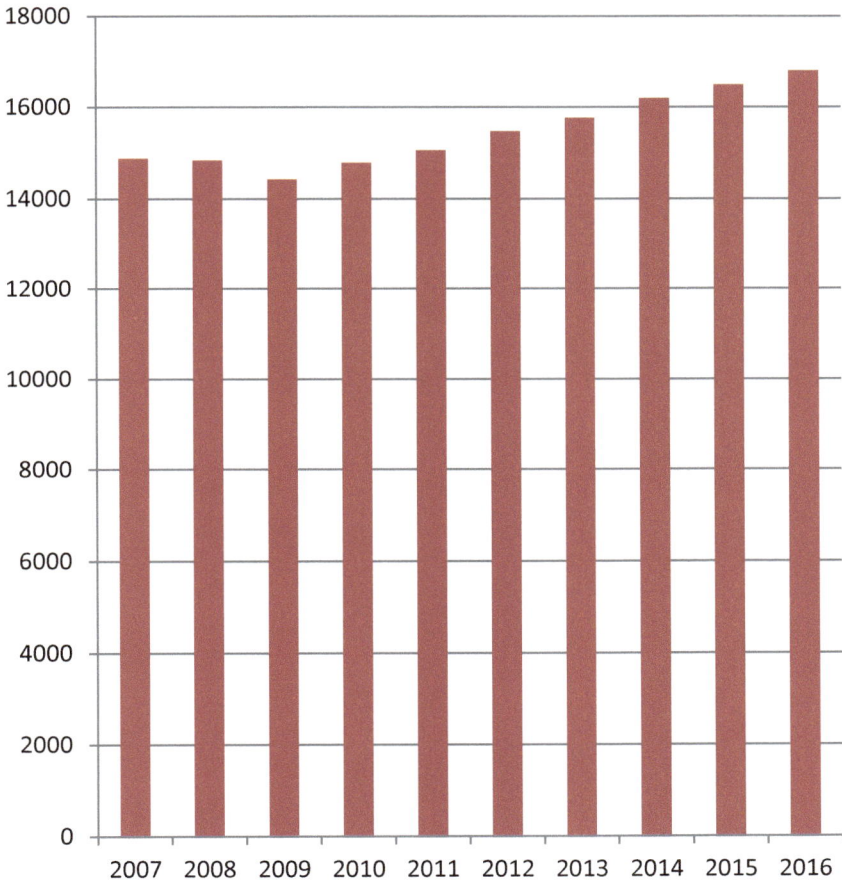

"Real" GDP in chained 2009 dollars.

---

6 www.bea.gov/National Income and product Accounts-Table1.1.6

If we compare the *accumulative percent* increase of M2 and GDP for the past eight years, it is apparent that the money supply has far outstripped the expansion of our Gross Domestic Product.

When the money supply expands faster than the ability of the economy to absorb it, pressure on pricing is created, leading to inflation. Inflation, in turn, results in higher interest rates. Higher interest rates drive up the cost of servicing our National Debt, leading to larger deficits. A vicious cycle indeed!

With interest rates at all time lows, the cost of servicing our National Debt is still a major factor in driving us deeper into negative Net Worth for the nation every year. Our legislators must be convinced to act now: waiting until it is obvious to them that action is required will leave the country in a precarious monetary position.

The following chart illustrates the disconnection between the Gross Domestic Product, GDP and the money supply, M2.

Values for this chart were calculated using the data from the websites noted for the previous charts for GDP and M2.

Accumulative Percentage Increase in M2 and GDP

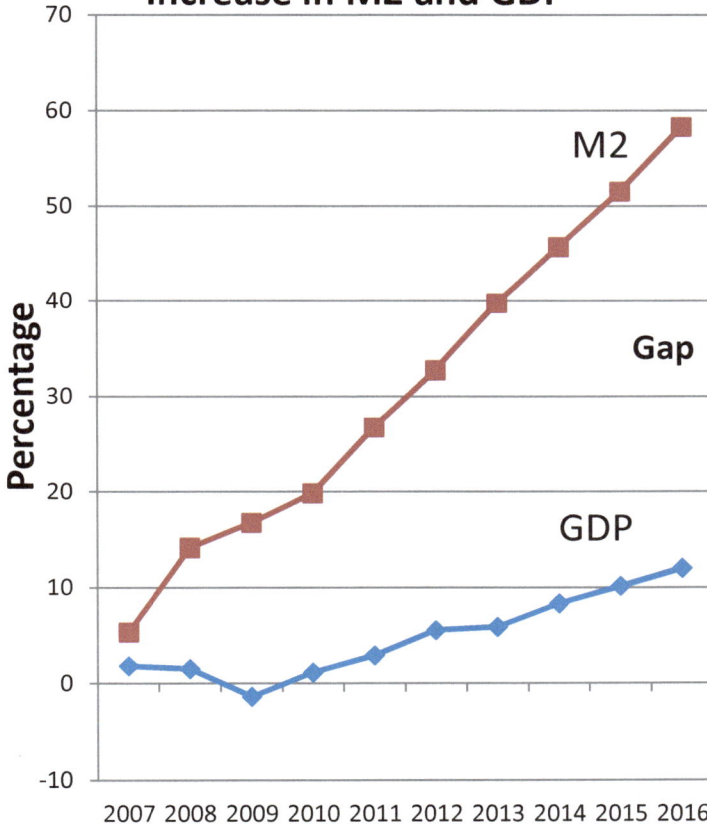

The flow of money into the economy is far outstripping the nations' ability to adequately absorb it. This condition has created a "GAP" between the rate of increase in M2 and the rate of increase in GDP. The relationship between increasing money supply, higher prices and higher interest rates is a simple matter of "cause and effect."

Gap = Inflation = Higher Interest Rates = Increased Deficits

What is it about the "GAP" that leads to inflation? It has its basis in the "Law of Supply and Demand". Postulated in 1691 by John Locke in his work, "Some Considerations of the Consequences of the Lowering of Interest and the Raising of the Value of Money", this economic truth has been established as an undeniable "cause and effect" relationship throughout the centuries that followed.

This age old truth states "When the demand for a product increases without a corresponding increase in supply, the price will rise.

In this case, supply is represented by the GDP and demand by the Money Supply, M2, in addition to the latent supply of excess reserves. Increasing the monetary base puts more money in the hands of the public without a corresponding increase in product availability, therefore causing an increase in price for the products which are available.

To better understand the connection between excess growth in Money Supply, (M/S), as compared to Gross Domestic Product,(GDP), refer to the following chart which shows the effect on prices when the supply, (GDP), remains constant, while the demand, (M/S), increases. In other words, the increase in the supply of money, without a corresponding increase in the availability of goods and services purchased with that money, will result in a rise in prices. (P2 – P1)

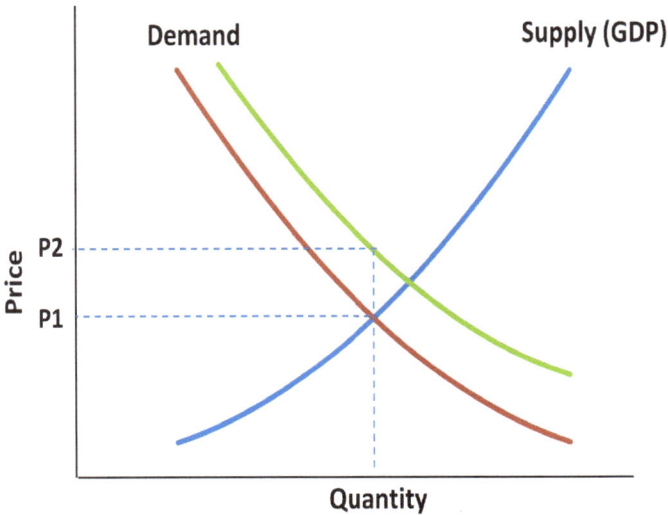

Supply and Demand Chart

As previously quoted from the Review by the Federal Reserve Bank of St. Louis: "EVERY MAJOR ACCELERATION IN M2 GROWTH HAS RESULTED IN INFLATION".

And why does this matter?

If you agree with the St. Louis Federal Reserve, inflation will inevitably follow the run up of our Money Stock relative to our Gross Domestic Product.

Inflation: *How is it measured?*

CPI:

The Consumer Price Index is the common indicator for inflation. The Bureau of Labor Statistics, United States Department of Labor, compiles the consumer price index and publishes it monthly.

Price indexes are available for the U.S., the four Census regions, size of city, cross-classifications of regions and size-classes, and for 26 local areas. Indexes are available for major groups of consumer expenditures (food and beverages, housing, apparel, transportation, medical care, recreation, education and communications, and other goods and services), for items within each group, and for special categories, such as services.

- Monthly indexes are available for the U.S., the four Census regions, and some local areas. More detailed item indexes are available for the U.S. than for regions and local areas.
- The CPI represents changes in prices of all goods and services purchased for consumption by urban households. User fees (such as water and sewer service) and sales and excise taxes paid by the consumer are also included.

- Prices for the goods and services used to calculate the CPI are collected in 87 urban areas throughout the country and from about 23,000 retail and service establishments. Data on rents are collected from about 50,000 landlords or tenants.

- Prices are taken throughout the month.

- As an economic indicator. As the most widely used measure of inflation, the CPI is an indicator of the effectiveness of government policy.

When there is more money available than goods and services to purchase, prices go up. Interest rates behave similarly. The cost of money is the interest you pay on the money you borrow. When prices are rising, lenders want higher rates of interest for their loans because they have more opportunities for their money.

To illustrate the correlation between inflation and interest rates, refer to the following chart of the Consumer Price Index and the Prime Rate of Interest. This chart shows the "cause and effect" relationship between CPI, (inflation), and interest rate.

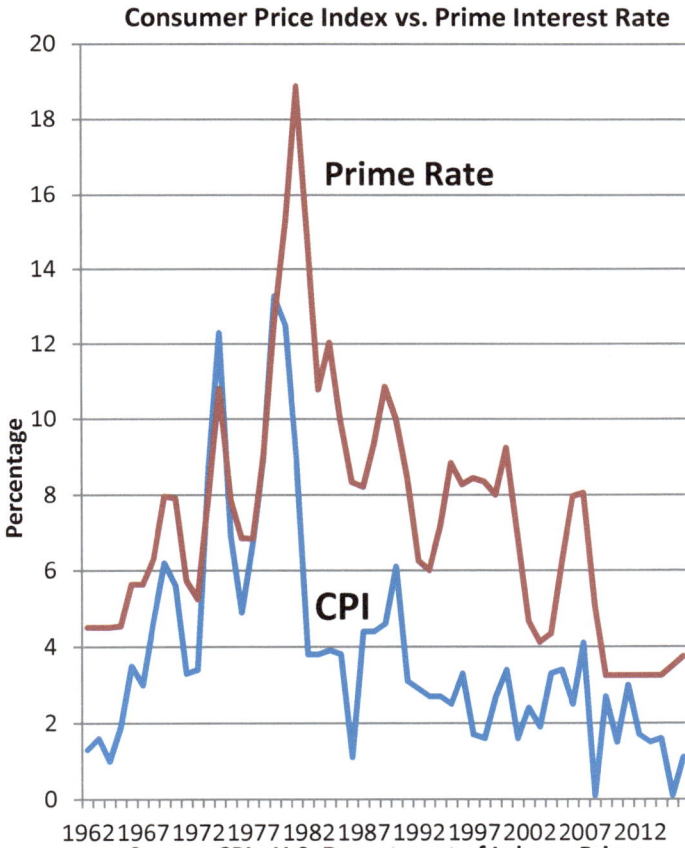

Consumer Price Index vs. Prime Interest Rate

Source: CPI - U.S. Department of Labor.   Prime
Rate - Board of Governors, Federal Reserve System

---

[7] U.S. Dept. of Labor: www.bls.gov/cpi/ Board of Governors, Federal Reserve System: www.federalreserve.gov/search.newyorkfed.org/

It can only be a matter of time before the pressure built-up by our money supply expansion results in increasing the rate of inflation. We have a relatively fixed amount of goods and services available, but we have a huge build up in money and excess reserves, inevitably resulting in bidding up prices.

So why does this matter?

Interest rates and inflation rates go hand in hand.

Congress appears to indulge the President in his desire to remove environmental restrictions on industry and spending on Defense and Infrastructure. When the "Trump Effect" takes hold, inflation will accelerate and become part of the public psyche. Once recognized, it will become a self-fulfilling phenomenon with prices and interest rates rising to unsafe levels. At this point the Fed will take action, but with history as our guide, it will be too little, too late. The damage will have been done. Interest on the National Debt could climb into double digits, which would be disastrous.

At the present time, with our debt over 19 Trillion Dollars, the interest cost represents 14.5% of our total receipts for the year, and that is at a rate for the past several years of only 2.4%. It is unrealistic to expect this interest rate to remain at this level for long. As the interest rate rises, it consumes more and more of the total income of the U.S.

The following chart shows the interest rate paid on the national debt from 1978 through 2016.

The data for this chart was obtained from the following sources: The U.S. Department of the Treasury at:
www.treasurydirect.gov/govt/reports/ir/ir_expense.htm

The United Stated General Accounting Office, (Report to the Secretary of the Treasury). www.gao.gov/assets/240/236271.pdf

Historical Average Interest Rate of Federal Debt Outstanding

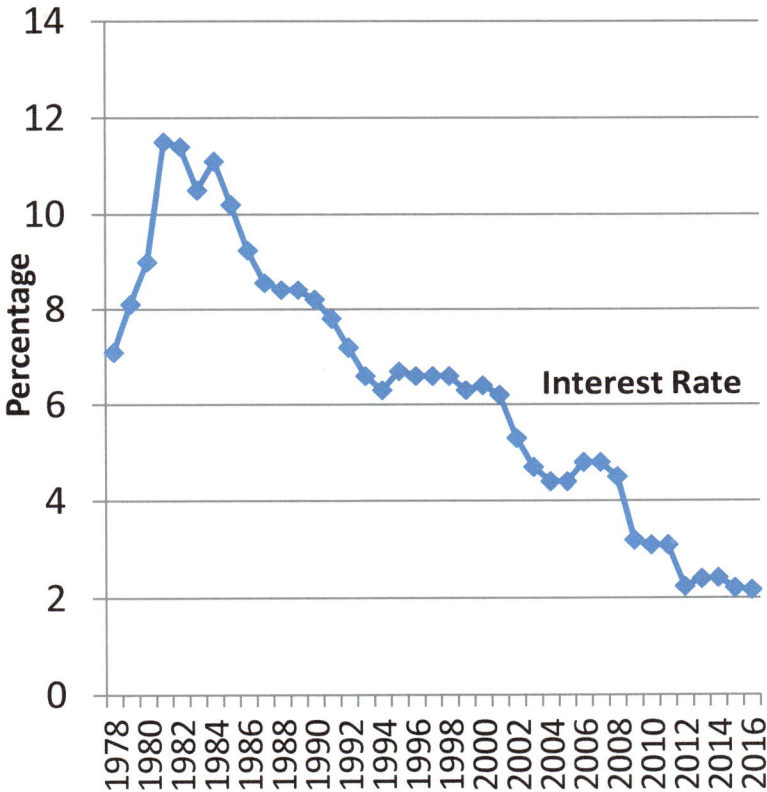

Source: U.S. Department of the Treasury

Our current rate of 2.4% results in a payment of 432,649,652,901.12. If the interest rate returned to 1983 levels, our yearly interest cost would exceed $ 2 TRILLION dollars. In other words, our interest cost on the national debt would consume more than half of our entire yearly budget! Keeping our country afloat would be extremely difficult under these circumstances.

Our national debt is going higher every day. The current amount of 19 Trillion dollars is completely unsustainable. The Federal Reserve will not be able to force down interest rates indefinitely, and when interest rates return to normal levels, we will be facing payments that will drive us into insolvency. If interest rates were to climb to 8% as they were in 1990, we would have to pay $ 1,594,825,200,000.in yearly interest cost. This amounts to one third of our total receipts. With total expenditures already exceeding receipts by over one trillion dollars, a spike in interest rates would send us over the edge. At this point, the Fed is "on the horns of a dilemma". If they continue to maintain interest rates at historic lows, they are only delaying the onset of the inevitable, but if they allow interest rates to rise, the cost of servicing our debt could become an impossible burden. The Fed is now in the position of "damned if they do, and damned if they don't.

Prior to the Feds action in 2008, the average interest rate paid by the Fed over the previous 20 years was 5.88%. At this average rate, the interest per year would be almost one trillion dollars. If the Trump's actions lead us into high inflation as they appear to be headed, the interest rate on the national debt could reach twelve per cent!

Remember:

Gap = Inflation = Higher Interest Rates = Increased Deficits

Cost of Interest on National Debt vs. Revenue

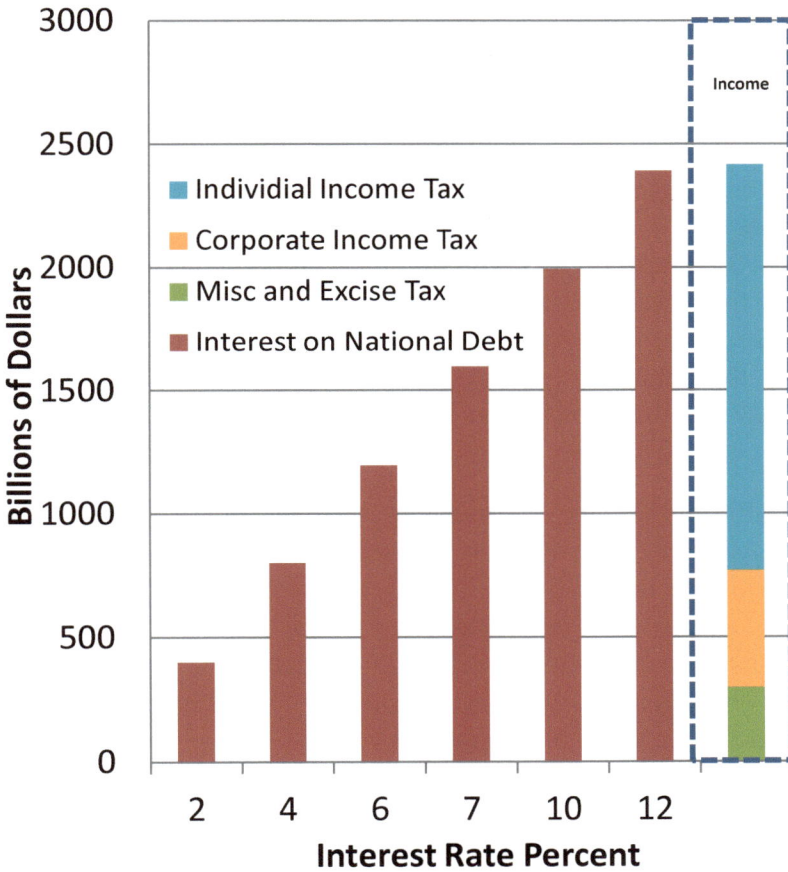

Legend:
- Individial Income Tax
- Corporate Income Tax
- Misc and Excise Tax
- Interest on National Debt

Y-axis: Billions of Dollars (0, 500, 1000, 1500, 2000, 2500, 3000)

X-axis: Interest Rate Percent (2, 4, 6, 7, 10, 12)

Income

This chart shows the income the Federal Government receives from various sources for 2016. Corporate Income and other taxes amount to 544 Billion dollars. Social Security Insurance Taxes bring in 986 Billion dollars while the Individual Income Tax accounts for 1.460 Trillion dollars.

The total of all revenue sources amount to 2.989 Trillion dollars for the U.S. Government for 2016.

Total expenditures for the year: 3.539 Trillion dollars.

Deficit for 2016: 550 Billion dollars.

By referring to the chart it can be seen that as the interest rate increases on the national debt, the yearly payment could exceed the total Corporate Income Tax Revenue, Miscellaneous and Excise Tax Revenue and the Individual Income Tax Revenue. Social Security Insurance Tax Revenue has been left out of this analysis since it can only be used for Social Security Purposes. It is conceivable that the interest cost could eventually consume every dollar of Total U.S. Revenue.

Eventually, the Federal Reserve is going to be unable to hold interest rates at the level of the past few years, and when the market decides that Treasury Bills at current interest rates do not warrant their money, interest rates will climb. As they do, banks will find better investments for their burgeoning reserves and this money will begin to flood out on the market, further exacerbating the predicament we find ourselves in.

Clearly we have a serious problem which cannot be pushed into the future. We must begin to reduce the debt.

The following chart of yearly surplus or deficit for the United States illustrates the situation we face.

Yearly Surplus (+) or Deficit (-) of the United States

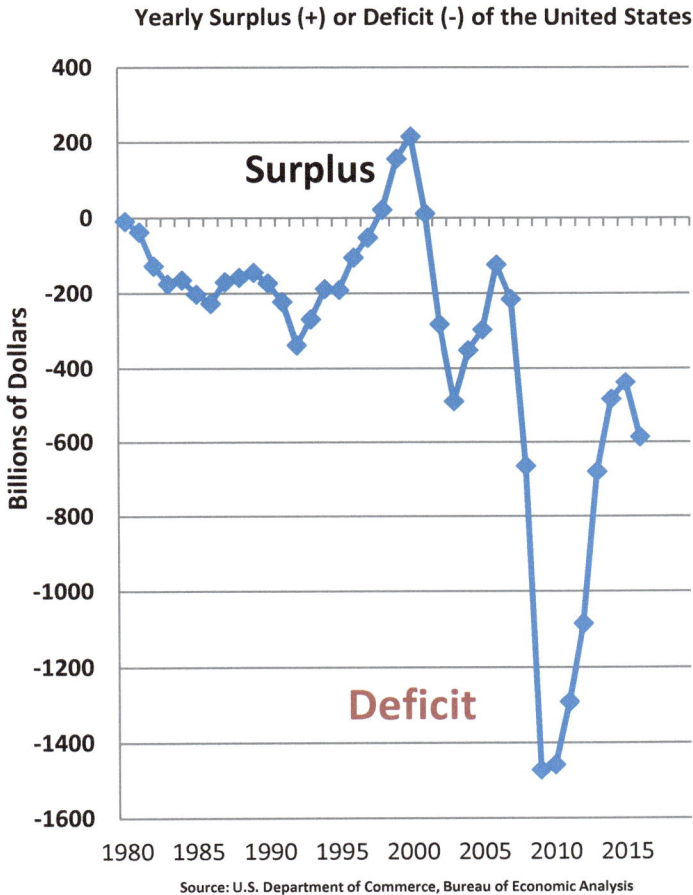

Source: U.S. Department of Commerce, Bureau of Economic Analysis

[1]http://www.bea.gov/national/nipaweb/Ni_FedBeaSna/TableView.asp?SelectedTable=7

The nations of the world are becoming nervous with their large dollar balances as they see the huge amount of excess reserves in our system while the Fed continues to pump more dollars into the economy. A devaluation of the dollar caused by inflation in the U.S. economy would be very unpleasant for them and they are beginning to question the stability of our great nation. This does not bode well for the future.

This is not a problem that can be solved by the Democrats alone, or the Republicans on their own, or any other political party. Partisan politics will not get this done. This is a problem that can only be resolved by Americans, working together, regardless of their party affiliation.

We need to act.

The deficit spending almost every year since 1980 has accumulated a negative net worth for our great nation which now exceeds Ten Trillion Dollars!

The following chart illustrates this fact.

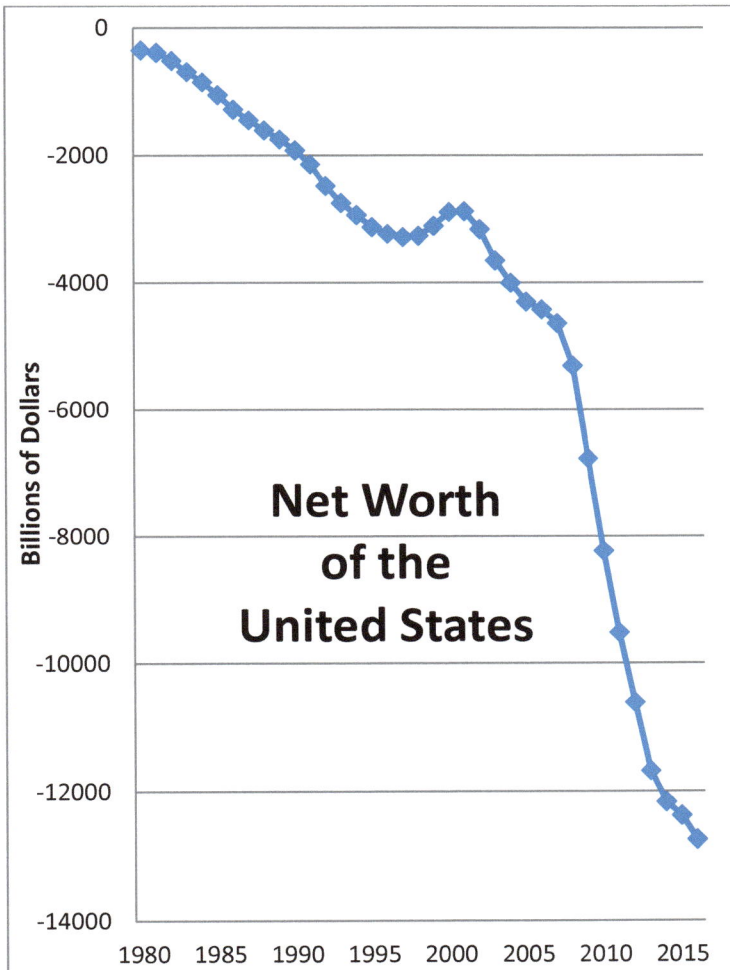

Net Worth of the United States

(Y-axis: Billions of Dollars, ranging from 0 to -14000; X-axis: years from 1980 to 2015)

1

http://www.bea.gov/national/nipaweb/Ni_FedBeaSna/TableView.asp?SelectedTable=7

There is a belief among many economists and those in government that the amount of our National Debt is immaterial as long as the ratio of our debt to the Gross Domestic Product is less than some magical percentage. This line of thinking is completely erroneous.

The ratio of National Debt that is meaningful is the total debt as a percentage of the income of the country. On this basis, with a total income of 3.248 Trillion dollars per year versus our debt of 19.9 Trillion dollars, the debt to income ratio is Six Hundred and Twelve Percent!

Another ratio we should be concerned with is the ratio of the cost of servicing our debt to our income. On this basis, at the current suppressed rate of 2.4%, this ratio is 15%. At an 8% interest rate, the cost of servicing our debt would be 30% of our total income!

With interest payments drawing off 30% of our income, the only recourse to providing the funds for our other commitments would be going further into debt. Reducing our expenses significantly is not going to happen. We must find the means to increase our income while we still have time.

Current Income Sources: Actual 2016 receipts, in Billions*

1.	Individual Income Taxes	1,460
2.	Social Insurance Taxes	986
3.	Corporate Income Taxes	262
4.	Other	281
	Total	2.989

Total Expenditures: Actual 2016, in Billions	3,539
Actual 2016 Deficit: in Billions	- 550

Source:*Executive Office of the President of the United States

We need to increase our income to bring us into equilibrium with our expenses.

Until we can scrutinize our entitlement programs and our military budget to determine where savings can be obtained, we must provide additional income.

"ANOTHER DAY OLDER AND DEEPER IN DEBT"

How did we manage to run up our debt to such an unmanageable amount? I think the simple answer is, we couldn't say NO. As demands for increased military budgets came along with the explanation that we had to spend the money for additional fire power and more troops because we had to protect the world from aggressors, the congress dutifully went along with the military. After trillions of dollars and untold number of shattered lives, are we really any better off? I think not. We must take care of business at home.

It wasn't just the military. As new social programs were proposed, congress found it difficult to vote against something that would benefit a large segment of the population. Besides, there was little argument against providing the poor with food stamps, or children with medical care, or the disabled with pensions. The argument should have focused on how the programs would be paid for.

We now have a conglomeration of programs which undeniably benefit a large number of the population, but are un-funded. Social Security and Medicare are the only federal social welfare programs which are partially self-funded. The remaining programs, and as we have seen, there are many, are not funded. Over the past eight years, our budget shortage per year has been between 400 Billion to 1.4 TRILLION dollars. In the song "Sixteen Tons" as sung by Tennessee Ernie Ford in 1955, "You load sixteen tons, what do you get, another day older and deeper in debt". This is the situation we are faced with today. We are working more but going deeper in debt. Nothing will change until we place people in government who believe in "biting the bullet" to help us out of this predicament.

You're thinking this isn't my problem. It's the government's problem, right? Well, we are the government and we are the problem. We have allowed our representatives in Washington to bury us with debt.

What can we do? After replacing Trump, reduce the military budget immediately to start cutting into our national debt.

How do we do it?

Elect representatives who understand the situation and have the courage to act.

The Fed's policy of low interest rates to stimulate the economy may be working too well. Unemployment is at historical lows and inflation is at their target rate. Problem is, interest rates are on the rise, and that means higher payments on the debt.

You might argue that if high inflation does occur, we can pay off the national debt with inflated dollars. This would be true, but interest rate increases would wipe out the benefit from inflated dollars.

Higher interest rates mean higher payments on the debt, which means higher budget deficits, which means higher debt – you get the idea?

The Fed won't let that happen, right? They'll take measures to correct the problem, just like they did for the housing crisis, right? We know how that went.

Without cutting expenses and increasing revenue, there is no way to extricate us from the mountain of debt that has accumulated.

If we can balance the budget while paying the interest on the debt, it will be a giant step forward.

This will all be politically difficult to say the least, but it must be done. It will require electing congressional candidates who understand the situation and have the courage to vote for fiscal responsibility.

Read what the Congressional Budget Office has to say about our debt in excerpts from their report:"The 2013 Long Term Budget Outlook". This analysis is still applicable today.

The 2013 Long-Term Budget Outlook

Report: September 17, 2013

*Between 2009 and 2012, the federal government recorded the largest budget deficits relative to the size of the economy since 1946, causing federal debt to soar. Federal debt held by the public is now about 73 percent of the economy's annual output, or gross domestic product (GDP). That percentage is higher than at any point in U.S. history except a brief period around World War II, and it is twice the percentage at the end of 2007. If current laws generally remained in place, federal debt held by the public would decline slightly relative to GDP over the next several years, CBO projects. After that, however, growing deficits would ultimately push debt back above its current high level. CBO projects that federal debt held by the public would reach 100 percent of GDP in 2038, 25 years from now, even without accounting for the harmful effects that growing debt would have on the economy (see the figure below). **Moreover, debt would be on an upward path relative to the size of the economy, a trend that could not be sustained indefinitely.***
Budget Projections for the Long Term: Looking beyond the 10-year period covered by its regular baseline projections, CBO produced an extended baseline for this report that extrapolates those projections through 2038 (and, with even greater uncertainty, through later decades). Under the extended baseline, budget deficits would rise steadily and, by 2038, would push federal debt held by the public close to the percentage of GDP seen just after World War II—even without factoring in the harm that growing debt would cause to the economy.

By 2038, CBO projects, federal spending would increase to 26 percent of GDP under the assumptions of the extended baseline, compared with 22 percent in 2012 and an average of 20½ percent over the past 40 years. That increase reflects the following projected paths for various types of federal spending if current laws generally remain in place (see the figure below):

- *Federal spending for the major health care programs and Social Security would increase to a total of 14 percent of GDP by 2038, twice the 7 percent average of the past 40 years.*
- *In contrast, total spending on everything other than the major health care programs, Social Security, and net interest payments would decline to 7 percent of GDP, well below the 11 percent average of the past 40 years and a smaller share of the economy than at any time since the late 1930s.*
- *The federal government's net interest payments would grow to 5 percent of GDP, compared with an average of 2 percent over the past 40 years, mainly because federal debt would be much larger.*

Harmful Effects of Large and Growing Debt

How long the nation could sustain such growth in federal debt is impossible to predict with any confidence. At some point, investors would begin to doubt the government's willingness or ability to pay U.S. debt obligations, making it more difficult or more expensive for the government to borrow money. Moreover, even before that point was reached, the high and rising amount of debt that CBO projects under the extended baseline would have significant negative consequences for both the economy and the federal budget:

- *Increased borrowing by the federal government would eventually reduce private investment in productive capital, because the portion of total savings used to buy government securities would not be available to finance private investment. The result would be a smaller stock of capital and lower output and income in the long run than would otherwise be the case. Despite those reductions, however, the continued growth of productivity would make real (inflation-adjusted) output and income per person higher in the future than they are now.*
- *Federal spending on interest payments would rise, thus requiring larger changes in tax and spending policies to achieve any chosen targets for budget deficits and debt.*
- *The government would have less flexibility to use tax and spending policies to respond to unexpected challenges, such as economic downturns or wars.*
- *The risk of a fiscal crisis—in which investors demanded very high interest rates to finance the government's borrowing needs—would increase.*

The Uncertainty of Long-Term Budget Projections

To illustrate the uncertainty of those projections, CBO examined how altering its assumptions about future productivity, interest rates, and federal spending on health care would affect the projections in the extended baseline. Under those alternative assumptions—which do not cover the full range of possible outcomes—federal debt held by the public in 2038 could range from as low as 65 percent of GDP (still elevated by historical standards) to as high as 156 percent of GDP, compared with the 108 percent of GDP projected under the extended baseline with the economic effects of fiscal policy included. Those calculations do not address other sources of uncertainty, such as the risk of an economic depression or major war or the possibility of unexpected changes in birth rates, life expectancy, immigration, or labor force participation. nonetheless, CBO's analysis shows that under a wide range of possible assumptions about some key factors that influence federal spending and revenues, **the budget is on an unsustainable path**.

Excerpt from the Congressional Budget Office - Report Dated Sept. 17, 2013, revised March 19, 2014:

"The gap between federal spending and revenues would widen steadily after 2015 under the assumptions of the extended baseline, CBO projects. By 2038, the deficit would be 6½ percent of GDP, larger than in any year between 1947 and 2008, and federal debt held by the public would reach 100 percent of GDP, more than in any year except 1945 and 1946. **With such large deficits, federal debt would be growing faster than GDP, a path that would ultimately be unsustainable.** *"* *end of quote

REMEMBER:
Gap = Inflation = Higher Interest Rates = Increased Deficits

How Bad Is It?

The Congressional Budget Office repeatedly refers to our budget path as "Unsustainable".

There is no easy way out. We must "bite the bullet". Entitlements should be scrutinized, the military budget reduced and income increased with a broad based tax. We cannot nibble at the edges, our situation demands surgery.

We did it before and we can do it again, we need to elect representatives who will make the hard choices.

There is no way the current tax structure could be tweaked to provide the amount of income we need to fund our entitlement programs and pay the interest on our debt. It has been a case of "same old, same old" for too many years. We can only do this by insuring that those we elect believe in these principles and have the fortitude to stand up for them.

We need to re-elect congressmen and women who have shown by their voting record that they vote with their conscience and not with their pocketbook.

We must end our obsession with converting the world to democracy and realize that nations are different. Everyone doesn't want what we want – it should not our mission to instigate change.

E Pluribus unum – "out of many, one" is an appropriate motto for a nation made up of many races and nationalities. We relish our freedom – we worship our freedom – we will defend our freedom – but we must stop trying to export our freedom. Nations must be left to find their own form of government that meets the needs of its citizens without foreign influence.

We need a new type of military – one that operates through global intelligence rather than ships and tanks and reduce the number of military personnel to that needed for defense. We should be able to meet our commitment with 45% of the current budget. Put our resources to work helping underprivileged citizens of the world by providing food and health care through mobile roaming land and sea facilities.

Income:

We need to replace the Income Tax with a GST (Goods and Services Tax)

How does our candidate feel about that?

Our current income sources leave us from 1/2 to a Trillion dollars short of meeting our commitments each year. We need to increase our income to bring us into equilibrium with our expenses. Our entitlement programs cannot be reduced in any meaningful manner. We must provide additional revenue to provide positive cash flow.

Increasing our income can be accomplished to some extent by scrutinizing our existing tax code for loopholes that benefit only a small percentage of the population. Congress has been fiddling around for years trying to find ways to eliminate tax loopholes and increase the marginal rate on income taxes, but has accomplished little. The most realistic way of providing sufficient income to solve our immediate problem is by instituting a consumer tax. Every nation of the world, with the exception of the United States, has a broad based consumer tax, known in most cases as a Value Added Tax, or VAT. The VAT is the primary source of income for many of the world's governments and its implementation in the U.S. is the logical choice for providing the amount of tax income we need. The VAT is a tax both Republicans and Democrats could agree on. Republicans because it would raise revenue, eliminate the budget deficit and it is not an income tax. Democrats could embrace it because it would solve the problem of funding entitlements and it is not regressive.

It is imperative that the candidates we support are in favor of paying down our debt by increasing our income through a Goods and Services Tax. Finding the right candidates is not going to be an easy job. Most politicians running for office consider endorsing additional taxes to be anathema to the electorate. We need bold, articulate candidates who are concerned for Humanity, Military excess, the National Debt and are unafraid to tackle the GST.

A model for us would be the broad based consumer tax established in New Zealand in 1986. By limiting the exemptions to the tax and simplifying the bookkeeping requirements, their version of the VAT, known as the GST – Goods and Services Tax - has proven to be one of the most successful variants of the VAT. The GST is a tax on most goods and services. The tax is added to the price of taxable goods and services at a rate of 15%. The only exceptions to the tax are renting a dwelling for use as a private home, interest payments you receive, donated goods sold by a non-profit and certain financial services. New Zealand's GST varies from other VAT's in that it is applied comprehensively at a single tax rate. There are no reduced rates, exemptions or zero-rates. Food, clothing, medical care, education services, energy and other necessities of life are taxed like all other goods and services.

Businesses add 15% to the price of goods they sell, but in turn, they are able to deduct the tax that was paid on the supplies they purchased. The tax is collected at each step in the supply chain. The manufacturer collects the tax on sales to wholesalers. The wholesalers collect the tax on sales to retailers and retailers pay the tax for products sold to consumers. A simplified example of how this works will be seen in the following table, calculated at a tax rate of 7.5%.

Consumer Tax under the GST Method:

	Manufacturer	Wholesaler	Retailer	Total Tax
Sales	400	700	1000	
Purchases	0	400	700	
Tax @ 7.5%	30	52.5	75	
Credit	0	30	52.5	
Tax Owed	30	22.5	22.5	75

In this example, it will be seen that the tax is distributed between the three entities involved, with the manufacturer paying a somewhat higher amount than the wholesaler and the retailer. This is obviously an over simplified illustration of the workings of the GST, but it shows the basic concept of how the tax and the tax credit is calculated.

New Zealand established the tax in 1986 at a 10% rate as a supplemental tax to their income tax. The New Zealand Income Tax ranges from 11.5% to 35.5%. The GST is currently at 15%

Based on estimates by the U.S. Department of Commerce, a broad based value added tax for the United States similar to the GST, at a tax rate of 7½% would generate over 824 Billion. Administrative costs for establishing and administering a GST for the U.S. would be from 5 to 8 Billion dollars, According to the Congressional Budget Office. Accounting for administrative costs and the inevitable exclusions to the tax which Congress would insert, the tax should net over 700 Billion for the U.S. This would enable us to begin paying down our debt before interest costs become overwhelming.

Instituting a 7.5% GST in America could mean eliminating the Income Tax as the debt is reduced.

VAT is not a regressive tax!

The argument against any broad based tax which taxes every citizen at the same rate is that it is regressive. That is, the lower income segment of the population, while paying the same rate of taxation as the higher income segment, is paying a higher percentage of their income in taxes. While this is true, there are several mitigating factors which are often overlooked in this discussion.

First: **Those with higher incomes are spending more than those with less, and therefore are paying more in total taxes than those with lower incomes, thereby subsidizing the lower income segment.**

Second: **Income should be considered over a lifetime rather than annually**. Income and consumption vary widely over a lifetime, with income varying more than consumption.

In a study of Annual vs. Lifetime Tax Burdens of Canadian Households, for income brackets from the lowest to the highest, the "regressive effect" of a broad based tax on consumption varied widely depending on whether the time frame was "Annual" or "Lifetime". This analysis shows that when the burden of a consumption tax was viewed over a lifetime, the regressive nature of the tax becomes negligible.

Income Bracket	Annual Tax Rate	Lifetime Tax Rate
Lowest	27.2	15.0
2	20.3	14.3
3	15.8	14.1
4	14.6	13.9
5	14.0	13.8
6	13.4	13.5
7	13.5	13.6
8	13.2	13.3
9	12.8	13.2
Highest	8.5	12.4

Source: Congressional Budget Office using data from James Davies, France St-Hilaire, and John Whalley, "Some Calculations of Lifetime Tax Incidence".

When you consider the small differences between the lowest income segment and the highest on a lifetime basis, and the fact that the higher income segment is paying more in total tax due to their higher spending, the "Regressive" argument against a consumption tax should be ended.

Third: **When you consider the yearly budget amount for entitlement spending of 2,657 Billion and the Total Budget Income of 3,033 Billion, 88% of the total income the United States receives from taxes is devoted to entitlement programs.** The recipients of our entitlement programs are, by and large, the very persons to whom we apply the regressive tax label. Considering where the money from taxes is spent, whether a tax is regressive or progressive is academic. If we want to continue to support our welfare programs, and I believe we do, we must pay for them. Each and every one of us, rich and poor, must pay for them.

Criticism of a broad based consumer tax is unjustified and cannot be defended on the basis of regressive tax analysis.

Some critics of the GST claim it would disrupt foreign trade, however recently, economist Paul Krugman, writing in the New York Times, said:

> "*Many people who should know better believe that value-added taxes, which many countries impose, discourage imports and subsidize exports. In fact, however, value-added taxes are basically national sales taxes, which neither discourage nor encourage imports. (Yes, imports pay the tax, but so do domestic products.)*"

Summary: Goods and Services Tax (GST)

GST in New Zealand is designed to be a broad based system with few exemptions.

End-users pay this tax on all liable goods and services indirectly, in that the purchase price of goods and services includes GST.

The existing rate for GST effective from 1 October 2010 is 15%.

NZ Income Tax at a glance

Personal income	33% from $70,000
	30%: $48,001 to $70,000
	17.5%: $14,001 to $48,000
	10.5%: $0 to $14,000

Company income   28%

Pie Chart illustrates total tax revenue for New Zealand:

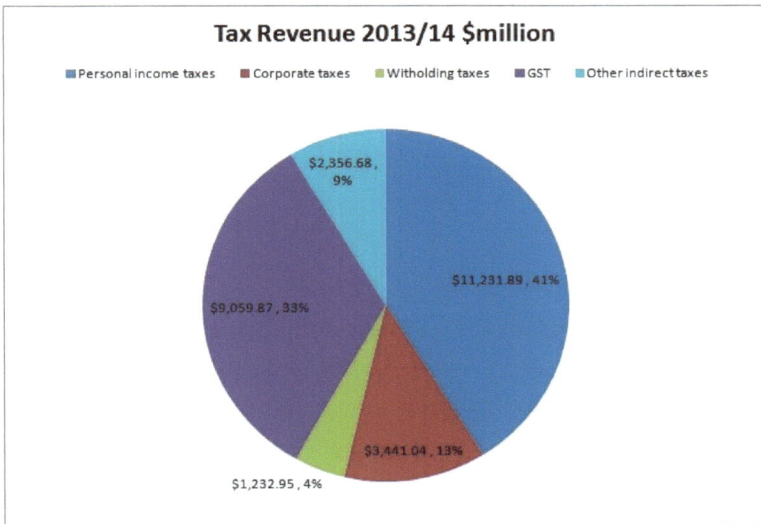

Tax Revenue 2013/14 $million

■ Personal income taxes   ■ Corporate taxes   ■ Witholding taxes   ■ GST   ■ Other indirect taxes

- $2,356.68, 9%
- $11,231.89, 41%
- $9,059.87, 33%
- $3,441.04, 13%
- $1,232.95, 4%

As distasteful as any additional tax may be, the specter of U.S. economic failure is much greater. Our current course is leading us inevitably to insolvency.

A tax similar to the Goods and Services Tax in New Zealand would provide the amount of income we require and would have the best chance to be enacted. The GST, combined with the reduction of the military budget, would bring us into a budget surplus.

This is tough medicine for what ails us, but the alternatives are a slow and agonizing death. As we are able to generate a surplus, our debt will retract and our interest costs will be reduced.

Current Budget		Projected Budget with a reduction in Military and addition of the GST:	
Military	604.5	Military	325.5
Other	3346.8	Other	3346.8
Total	3951.3	Total	3672.3
Income	3335.5	Income	4035.5
Deficit	615.8	Surplus	363.2

With the reduction in Military expenses of 279 Billion and the addition of 700 Billion to our receipts from the GST, we would convert a 615.8 Billion Dollar Deficit into a 363.2 Billion Dollar Surplus while still meeting all of our Entitlement commitments. Reducing the National Debt by 363 Billion Dollars would begin the cycle of reducing interest costs on the debt allowing us to begin reducing the Income Tax proportionately, enabling us to eventually eliminate the Income Tax.

When our world partners see that we are serious about controlling our finances, concern for the longevity of the U.S. government will abate and pressure on our dollar will diminish. The longer we continue down the path of budget deficits and increasing debt the more difficult our job will become.

We need political candidates who are not necessarily Democratic or Republican, but are committed to a reconfigured military force and financial programs which will bring health back into our finances.

Being concerned about the welfare of our citizens is not Socialism, it is Humanitarianism.

It is no longer a question of should we support our social programs, but it is a question of how do we support these programs. It is unfortunate that we have allowed ourselves to go so deeply in debt, as it is the interest cost on that debt that saps the income that could be spent on sustaining our entitlement programs.

We must recognize that cutting back on Social Security, Medicare, Medicaid, Health Insurance, Child Welfare, Pensions for government workers and military personnel, Income security for veterans, Educational subsidies and Farm subsidies is not possible.

At this point, we have to tighten our belts in order to pay off our debt and return to a "pay as you go" budget. We can do it if we reduce the military budget and increase our income by adding the GST.

Since there is no hope of accomplishing this with Trump in the White House, our first priority must be to blunt his programs until we can replace him as our President by 2020 or sooner.

Let's get to work!

APPENDIX

Common Sense is a pamphlet written by Thomas Paine. It was first published anonymously on January 10, 1776, at the beginning of the American Revolution. *Common Sense*, signed "Written by an Englishman", became an immediate success.

Being a part of Britain would drag America into unnecessary European wars, and keep it from the international commerce at which America excelled.

Much hath been said of the united strength of Britain and the Colonies, that in conjunction they might bid defiance to the world. But this is mere presumption; the fate of war is uncertain, neither do the expressions mean anything; for this continent would never suffer itself to be drained of inhabitants, to support the British arms in either Asia, Africa, or Europe.

Besides, what have we to do with setting the world at defiance? Our plan is commerce, and that, well attended to, will secure us the peace and friendship of all Europe; because it is the interest of all Europe to have America a free port. Her trade will always be a protection, and her barrenness of gold and silver secure her from invaders.

I challenge the warmest advocate for reconciliation to show a single advantage that this continent can reap by being connected with Great Britain. I repeat the challenge; not a single advantage is derived. Our corn will fetch its price in any market in Europe, and our imported goods must be paid for buy them where we will.

But the injuries and disadvantages which we sustain by that connection, are without number; and our duty to mankind at large, as well as to ourselves, instruct us to renounce the alliance: because, any submission to, or dependence on, Great Britain, tends directly to involve this Continent in European wars and quarrels, and set us at variance with nations who would otherwise seek our friendship, and against whom we have neither anger nor complaint. As Europe is our market for trade, we ought to form no partial connection with any part of it. It is the true interest of America to steer clear of European contentions, which she never can do, while, by her dependence on Britain, she is made the makeweight in the scale of British politics.

The Declaration of Independence:

IN CONGRESS, July 4, 1776.

The unanimous Declaration of the thirteen united States of America,

When in the Course of human events, it becomes necessary for one people to dissolve the political bands which have connected them with another, and to assume among the powers of the earth, the separate and equal station to which the Laws of Nature and of Nature's God entitle them, a decent respect to the opinions of mankind requires that they should declare the causes which impel them to the separation.

We hold these truths to be self-evident, that all men are created equal, that they are endowed by their Creator with certain unalienable Rights, that among these are Life, Liberty and the pursuit of Happiness.--That to secure these rights, Governments are instituted among Men, deriving their just powers from the consent of the governed, --That whenever any Form of Government becomes destructive of these ends, it is the Right of the People to alter or to abolish it, and to institute new Government, laying its foundation on such principles and organizing its powers in such form, as to them shall seem most likely to effect their Safety and Happiness. Prudence, indeed, will dictate that Governments long established should not be changed for light and transient causes; and accordingly all experience hath shewn, that mankind are more disposed to suffer, while evils are sufferable, than to right themselves by abolishing the forms to which they are accustomed. But when a long train of abuses and usurpations, pursuing invariably the same Object evinces a design to reduce them under absolute Despotism, it is their right, it is their duty, to throw off such Government, and to provide new Guards for their future security.--Such has been the patient sufferance of these Colonies; and such is now the necessity which constrains them to alter their former Systems of Government. The history of the present King of Great Britain is a history of repeated injuries and usurpations, all having in direct object the establishment of an absolute Tyranny over these States. To prove this, let Facts be submitted to a candid world.

He has refused his Assent to Laws, the most wholesome and necessary for the public good.
He has forbidden his Governors to pass Laws of immediate and pressing importance, unless suspended in their operation till his Assent should be obtained; and when so suspended, he has utterly neglected to attend to them.

He has refused to pass other Laws for the accommodation of large districts of people, unless those people would relinquish the right of Representation in the Legislature, a right inestimable to them and formidable to tyrants only.
He has called together legislative bodies at places unusual, uncomfortable, and distant from the depository of their public Records, for the sole purpose of fatiguing them into compliance with his measures.
He has dissolved Representative Houses repeatedly, for opposing with manly firmness his invasions on the rights of the people.
He has refused for a long time, after such dissolutions, to cause others to be elected; whereby the Legislative powers, incapable of Annihilation, have returned to the People at large for their exercise;

the State remaining in the mean time exposed to all the dangers of invasion from without, and convulsions within.

He has endeavoured to prevent the population of these States; for that purpose obstructing the Laws for Naturalization of Foreigners; refusing to pass others to encourage their migrations hither, and raising the conditions of new Appropriations of Lands.

He has obstructed the Administration of Justice, by refusing his Assent to Laws for establishing Judiciary powers.

He has made Judges dependent on his Will alone, for the tenure of their offices, and the amount and payment of their salaries.

He has erected a multitude of New Offices, and sent hither swarms of Officers to harrass our people, and eat out their substance.

He has kept among us, in times of peace, Standing Armies without the Consent of our legislatures.

He has affected to render the Military independent of and superior to the Civil power.

He has combined with others to subject us to a jurisdiction foreign to our constitution, and unacknowledged by our laws; giving his Assent to their Acts of pretended Legislation:

For Quartering large bodies of armed troops among us:

For protecting them, by a mock Trial, from punishment for any Murders which they should commit on the Inhabitants of these States:

For cutting off our Trade with all parts of the world:

For imposing Taxes on us without our Consent:

For depriving us in many cases, of the benefits of Trial by Jury:

For transporting us beyond Seas to be tried for pretended offences

For abolishing the free System of English Laws in a neighbouring Province, establishing therein an Arbitrary government, and enlarging its Boundaries so as to render it at once an example and fit instrument for introducing the same absolute rule into these Colonies:

For taking away our Charters, abolishing our most valuable Laws, and altering fundamentally the Forms of our Governments:

For suspending our own Legislatures, and declaring themselves invested with power to legislate for us in all cases whatsoever.

He has abdicated Government here, by declaring us out of his

Protection and waging War against us.

He has plundered our seas, ravaged our Coasts, burnt our towns, and destroyed the lives of our people.

He is at this time transporting large Armies of foreign Mercenaries to compleat the works of death, desolation and tyranny, already begun with circumstances of Cruelty & perfidy scarcely paralleled in the most barbarous ages, and totally unworthy the Head of a civilized nation.

He has constrained our fellow Citizens taken Captive on the high Seas to bear Arms against their Country, to become the executioners of their friends and Brethren, or to fall themselves by their Hands.

He has excited domestic insurrections amongst us, and has endeavoured to bring on the inhabitants of our frontiers, the merciless Indian Savages, whose known rule of warfare, is an undistinguished destruction of all ages, sexes and conditions.

In every stage of these Oppressions We have Petitioned for Redress in the most humble terms: Our repeated Petitions have been answered only by repeated injury. A Prince whose character is thus marked by every act which may define a Tyrant, is unfit to be the ruler of a free people.

Nor have We been wanting in attentions to our Brittish brethren. We have warned them from time to time of attempts by their legislature to extend an unwarrantable jurisdiction over us. We have reminded them of the circumstances of our emigration and settlement here. We have appealed to their native justice and magnanimity, and we have conjured them by the ties of our common kindred to disavow these usurpations, which, would inevitably interrupt our connections and correspondence. They too have been deaf to the voice of justice and of consanguinity. We must, therefore, acquiesce in the necessity, which denounces our Separation, and hold them, as we hold the rest of mankind, Enemies in War, in Peace Friends.

We, therefore, the Representatives of the united States of America, in General Congress, Assembled, appealing to the Supreme Judge of the world for the rectitude of our intentions, do, in the Name, and by Authority of the good People of these Colonies, solemnly publish and declare, That these United Colonies are, and of Right ought to be Free and Independent States; that they are Absolved from all Allegiance to the British Crown, and that all political connection between them and the State of Great Britain, is and ought to be totally dissolved; and that as Free and Independent States, they have full Power to levy War, conclude Peace, contract Alliances, establish Commerce, and to do all other Acts and Things which Independent States may of right do. And for the support of this Declaration, with a firm reliance on the protection of divine Providence, we mutually pledge to each other our Lives, our Fortunes and our sacred Honor.

Excerpts from

The Constitution of the United States

Preamble

We the People of the United States, in Order to form a more perfect Union, establish Justice, insure domestic Tranquility, **provide for the common defence**, promote the general Welfare, and secure the Blessings of Liberty to ourselves and our Posterity, do ordain and establish this Constitution for the United States of America.

Article I. - The Legislative Branch

Section 8 - Powers of Congress

To define and punish Piracies and Felonies committed on the high Seas, and Offenses against the Law of Nations; To declare War, grant Letters of Marque and Reprisal, and make Rules concerning Captures on Land and Water; To raise and support Armies, but no Appropriation of Money to that Use shall be for a longer Term than two Years; To provide and maintain a Navy; To make Rules for the Government and Regulation of the land and naval Forces; To provide for calling forth the Militia to execute the Laws of the Union, suppress Insurrections and repel Invasions; To provide for organizing, arming, and disciplining the Militia, and for governing such Part of them as may be employed in the Service of the United States, reserving to the States respectively, the Appointment of the Officers, and the Authority of training the Militia according to the discipline prescribed by Congress.

Article II. - The Executive Branch
Section 1 - The President
Section 2 - Civilian Power over Military, Cabinet, Pardon Power, Appointments

The President shall be Commander in Chief of the Army and Navy of the United States, and of the Militia of the several States, when called into the actual Service of the United States; he may require the Opinion, in writing, of the principal Officer in each of the executive Departments, upon any subject relating to the Duties of their respective Offices, and he shall have Power to Grant Reprieves and Pardons for Offenses against the United States, except in Cases of Impeachment.

The Amendments

The following are the Amendments to the Constitution. The first ten Amendments collectively are commonly known as the Bill of Rights.

First Amendment

Congress shall make no law respecting an establishment of religion, or prohibiting the free exercise thereof; or abridging the freedom of speech, or of the press, or the right of the people peaceably to assemble, and to petitition the Government for a redress of grievances.

Second Amendment

A well regulated Militia, being necessary to the security of a free State, the right of the people to keep and bear Arms, shall not be infringed.

Third Amendment

No Soldier shall, in time of peace be quartered in any house, without the consent of the Owner; nor in time of war, but in a manner to be prescribed by law.

Fourth Amendment

The right of the people to be secure in their persons, houses, papers, and effects, against unreasonable searches and seizures, shall not be violated, and no Warrants shall issue, but upon probable cause, supported by Oath or affirmation, and particularly describing the place to be searched, and the persons or things to be seized.

Fifth Amendment

No person shall be held to answer for a capital, or otherwise infamous crime, unless on a presentment or indictment of a Grand Jury, except in cases arising in the land or naval forces, or in the Militia, when in actual service in time of War or public danger; nor shall any person be subject for the same offence to be twice put in jeopardy of life or limb; nor shall be compelled in any criminal case to be a witness against himself; nor be deprived of life, liberty, or property, without due process of law; nor shall private property be taken for public use without just compensation.

Sixth Amendment

In all criminal prosecutions, the accused shall enjoy the right to a speedy and public trial, by an impartial jury of the State and district wherein the crime shall have been committed; which district shall have been previously ascertained by law, and to be informed of the nature and cause of the accusation; to be confronted with the witnesses against him; to have compulsory process for obtaining witnesses in his favor; and to have the assistance of counsel for his defence.

Seventh Amendment

In Suits at common law, where the value in controversy shall exceed twenty dollars, the right of trial by jury shall be preserved, and no fact tried by a jury shall be otherwise reexamined in any Court of the United States, than according to the rules of common law.

Eighth Amendment

Excessive bail shall not be required, nor excessive fines imposed, nor cruel and unusual punishments inflicted.

Ninth Amendment

The enumeration in the Constitution of certain rights shall not be construed to deny or disparage others retained by the people.

Tenth Amendment

The powers not delegated to the United States by the Constitution, nor prohibited by it to the States, are reserved to the States respectively, or to the people.

Author:

Carl Wray Hilton was born in Chicago, Illinois and grew up in Detroit, Michigan. As a teenager, he worked in the manufacturing plants of Hudson Motor Car Company and Chrysler Corporation. He joined the Naval Air Corps and served in the U.S. Navy until the end of World War II. Carl graduated from M.I.T. with a degree in Economics and Engineering and later earned an MBA from the University of Chicago.

Carl's entire career has been creating and managing manufacturing and distribution businesses.
His first business venture was as a distributer for the Oilite Division of Chrysler Corporation. This business led to distributing a full line of industrial products and the acquisition of a bronze foundry in Minneapolis.

Carl built a manufacturing plant in Arlington Heights, Illinois for the continuous casting of Bronze and Aluminum Bronze. He also founded a Powdered Metal factory in Muskegon, Michigan for the production of automotive and appliance parts.

In his Muskegon and Minneapolis factories, Carl worked with representatives of the International Machinists Union to provide for the welfare of his employees in addition to establishing a profit sharing program in which all of his employees participated.

Carl has supported every United States President from Franklin D. Roosevelt to Barack Obama. He has never openly criticized a sitting President. This changed with the election of Donald J. Trump. Carl feels this President is the antithesis of everything our country stands for. To remain quiet in the face of atrocities against the American people would be criminal and it is why he felt compelled to write this book.

www.ingramcontent.com/pod-product-compliance
Lightning Source LLC
Chambersburg PA
CBHW041225270326
41933CB00006B/212